D0121761

It gives me pleasure to recommend to you Hungry for Happiness, *a genuinely useful (and entertaining) book about discovering the weight that feels right for you. Samantha Skelly is the perfect kind of guide for your journey: She's been there, and she radiates the kind of clarity and compassion you can only get from dealing with weight struggles yourself. I've been there, too. As readers of my books know, I was an obese child who was taken to numerous medical specialists to find out why I was the fat kid in a family where everybody else was skinny. I was put on various regimens, but nothing really solved the problem until I had an awakening of consciousness when I was 24 years old. I turned my gaze inward, instead of outward toward trying a new diet every few months. What I discovered on my inward journey changed my life profoundly; within a year I lost more than 100 pounds and have kept it off ever since. Samantha went on a similar journey, but from a very different direction. (Hint: I never looked like a bikini model!) No matter what your shape, though, there are words of wisdom for you throughout the book. She discovered, as I did, that handling your weight issues is as much a spiritual practice as it is physical or emotional. It is my hope that* Hungry for Happiness *will find its way into the hands of millions of people who are suffering from the many difficulties that come from a troubled relationship with food. Wherever you are in this process, I think you will find Samantha's book a source of wisdom and a healing for your heart.*

— **Gay Hendricks, Ph.D., author of** *The Big Leap* **and** *Conscious Luck*

HUNGRY
FOR
HAPPINESS

REVISED & UPDATED

HUNGRY
FOR
HAPPINESS

Stop Emotional Eating
& Start Loving Yourself

SAMANTHA SKELLY

HAY HOUSE, INC.
Carlsbad, California • New York City
London • Sydney • New Delhi

Library of Congress Cataloging-in-Publication Data

Names: Skelly, Samantha, author.
Title: Hungry for happiness : stop emotional eating & start loving yourself / Samantha Skelly.
Description: 1st. edition., revised and updated. | Carlsbad, California : Hay House, Inc., 2020.
Identifiers: LCCN 2020026111 | ISBN 9781401957728 (hardback) | ISBN 9781401957742 (ebook)
Subjects: LCSH: Compulsive eating. | Compulsive eaters--United States--Biography.
Classification: LCC RC552.C65 S54 2020 | DDC 616.85/26--dc23
LC record available at https://lccn.loc.gov/2020026111

Hardcover ISBN: 978-1-4019-5772-8
E-book ISBN: 978-1-4019-5774-2
Audiobook ISBN: 978-1-4019-5773-5

10 9 8 7 6 5 4 3 2 1
1st edition, September 2020

Printed in the United States of America

✦ ✦ ✦

This book is for you:
the brave soul reading these words,
searching for the truth and deeper healing.
Please borrow my belief in you until
you feel it within you.
I see you.

✦ ✦ ✦

CONTENTS

FOREWORD

I knew in my soul the weight on my body was a representation of the physical weight I was holding on to for years. My avoidance to look at the weight through the lens of love and listen to what it needed kept it bonded to my body for years

I knew deep down what the weight was mirroring internally and how it was trying to keep me safe

For years of my life I wore a jacket. That jacket looked like 78 pounds of additional weight. I wore this jacket for comfort, but—what it really represented was a false sense of security that distanced me from my truth. The pain of my past, the pain of my son's father being in prison, the pain and worry I had for my son's future.

The weigh held me down. I stuffed down the agony of the truth until I was ready to unearth the hurt, love it fiercely, and release it once and for all.

Releasing this weight allowed me to land back on earth. It allowed me to feel deeply into the body I had been at war with for years and remember a felt sense of love for myself that was always there, yet had been muted by the weight.

I started praying for guidance. I said, *God, how can I be more responsible and lead in a better way?* I felt the spirit whisper to me: *Design your body so it lives out your life's purpose.* The message came in so clear.

One day, a good friend asked me, "Why don't you address this pain?" I thought about the idea and my entire body contracted. "If I lie down and cry, I don't think I will ever get up, this pain has been cured deep within me for 20 years."

"Trust yourself," he said. And I did; the path began.

My path of releasing my emotional and physical weight was a journey that brought me closer to my soul, my purpose, and my body—this journey was potent with gifts from the universe that allowed me to experience my truth on a deeper level. This is my deepest wish for you, and for all women.

Hungry for Happiness will destroy and break away the parts of you that are holding you back from your truth and awaken the parts of you that have been forgotten. Samantha will guide you on a journey to find deep peace in the places within yourself you've been resistant to visit.

If you let it, this book will move you to places that feel like home, the places your soul has been begging you to visit. You'll embark on a path back into your body, the infinite seat of love where peace prevails and all else falls away.

Grab a cozy blanket and a cup of tea and devour this piece of work. This is your time.

Lisa Nichols, motivational speaker, CEO, and
New York Times best-selling author

INTRODUCTION
by Way of Invitation

When I was a kid, I went on a 12-day road trip with my family. Yes, 12 days in a car with my disaster-prone family with nothing to do but listen to each other and our meager collection of cassette tapes. By day four, the open Saskatchewan highways remained unchanging for miles and miles. I would fall asleep and wake up hours later to the exact same scene: harvest fields for as far as my eyes could see in both directions, blue skies, and wisps of clouds. The old joke is when your dog runs away, you can watch him go for days in places like that. I believe it.

As I watched the multicolored sunset paint the night sky, I listened to a tape Dad popped in when everyone was sleeping. I could hear this man's raspy, passionate voice straining through the speakers in my dad's 1992 Ford Aerostar van. It was Tony Robbins. I listened, taking in each word.

At that point in my life, I was a terrible student. I resisted authority and spent most of my days sitting in the back of the class and mapping out business plans for the dance studio I was going to open. When my teachers would call on me for an answer, I'd say: "I'm not sure, and that probably won't help my life path—can you ask someone else?" I was such a little shit, but all I wanted to do in high school was dance, attend drama class, and build mini businesses. That was all I cared about, and I just didn't see the point of history or chemistry. I can remember Dad saying to me, "Don't worry about it—the A+ students end up working for the C students," and "You're an entrepreneur, school isn't set up for you."

This gave me all the permission I needed, so I tried just enough in school to not fail.

Tony Robbins screamed phrases like: "You can change your state in an instant!" "You are in complete control of your emotions!" "Your emotions are life!" and "Change your emotions and change your life!" over the car radio.

Okay, Tony, tell me more. I'm all ears, bro.

A lot of what he was saying didn't make sense to my young 14-year-old ears, but I listened. At this point, I had already started down my path of body image issues, but I wasn't yet consciously aware of them as a problem. And there *were* things I liked about myself. During high school I found myself internally rolling my eyes at the teen drama and silly conversations, even as I joined in—at 14, not fitting in was basically the same as death. Still, I always felt different, like I never truly belonged in high school. While most of my girlfriends were busy making out with boys, sneaking alcohol, and stealing their parents' cars after midnight, I was at home, sober as a judge, writing out my goals, creating business plans, and practicing my dance routines.

The sky was a deep blue by then, and as the moon was rising over the flat fields all I could hear was Tony's voice and the sound of cars whipping by. Everyone was sleeping except Dad and me, although he didn't know I was awake. This was one of those moments, when the air feels electric with possibility. I felt alive. The tape ended and all I could see were the oncoming headlights and the nearly full moon shining down on the fields. I drifted off to sleep.

Twelve years later I woke up in a pile of garbage from my latest binge on junk food. I've never been a big drinker, but I've been around enough alcoholics to hear people talk about this rock bottom moment when you sort of wake up and realize the mess you've gotten yourself into. This was my version of a moment of clarity: Two empty chip bags, a bottle of Diet Coke, and a half-eaten bar of Cadbury chocolate were strewn around me on the couch. These moments post-binge felt like the worst place I could possibly be. My inner critic was so loud in my head, blaring at me over a bullhorn and so cruel I could cry.

These binges made me feel like I was in a trance, like I was drugged. It's almost as if I'd lost all concept of what I was doing, these powerful emotions driving me into behaviors that were so out of alignment with my truth that I barely knew the person who was in my body. Who was this person eating all of this food? As I sat there in my apartment, the memory of being in the car with my dad listening to Tony Robbins came back to me suddenly. The second I reflected on this moment, Tony's words rang in my ears. I began to ask: *How did I get myself so lost in the mess?* This struggle with food and my body had stolen my light and my hope. It barely made any sense. Where was my inner 14-year-old? The one who valued personal development over grades and high school crushes? The one who was committed to finding happiness and to being the life of the party?

I wanted her back. I wanted to be her again. I wanted to savor the moment and live like I didn't have a care in the world, when joy was my only goal. Where was she?

I fell into the memory of that night in the car, the peace I felt in the moment of complete flow and utter ease. My inner critic went silent. "Your life is determined by your emotions." Tony's words burned into my brain, and I began to think of all the times I found myself face down in my own tears, ashamed.

For years, I'd inadvertently let my emotions run the show, like a half-naked toddler running wild, screaming, with a trail of destruction in her wake. I had no control of my emotions. They dictated everything because, ironically, I was trying so hard to control them I couldn't feel or see anything else. I chucked the evidence of the previous night's binge into the garbage, grabbed my journal, and began to get clear on where I was and where I wanted to be. I was nowhere near there, but with Tony's words echoing in my memory, it was a start.

What I understood that day is that everything you need is within you right now. Everything you need to make yourself feel horrendous or wonderful. Everything you need to make yourself feel freedom, peace, and ease, or anxiety and upset. It's all there. You get to choose the path.

✦ ✦ ✦

It took me years to learn the lessons I write about in this book, and I am writing it to share what I have learned so that women like me, caught in the cycle, can begin the healing journey sooner rather than later.

This book is for women who want to reclaim their power and fall in love with their bodies. This book is for women who want to say "fuck it" to dieting. This book is for women who know they were designed for more and built for more—filled with potential just waiting to be discovered. This book is for women who want to end their battle with food. This book is for women who are craving joy. This book is for women who want to feel alive again.

And here is a thing you might not know yet: Your relationship with food is a blessing.

I know you're thinking, *Sam, that's not true. My fight with food is eating me alive, literally.* And yes, I know exactly how you are feeling because that is exactly how I felt before I recognized my own inherent worth and started to live from that truth. Before I found a way out, I lived in a diet depression for years of my life. I know what that battle feels like—a constant war in your mind. There were days I wanted to crawl out of my skin and into a hole to hide away from the world. I had a voice in my head that didn't shut up, no matter how much I tried to distract myself with puppy videos on Facebook or overexercising. I get you, girl. I see you. I feel you. I was you.

But there is a way out. And if I am more honest, it is not a way out at all but a way in. A way into the relationship with your body and food that you have been craving for a very long time. I know what a struggle it feels like, and if I can make this happen, so can you. Your struggle is my struggle, my freedom is your freedom. We are on this journey together: coexisting, growing, and expanding into the highest, best, and most authentic versions of ourselves.

You're searching for a remedy, an escape, an answer to the battle you've created in your mind. You are looking for a way off this constantly changing carousel, this vicious cycle you're in with food and your body. This book is it. This is your answer.

I want you to know something, my fellow warrior: The battle you're in is temporary. The battle you're in will soon become the catalyst to your growth. I know that it might seem impossible right now, but your battle will soon become a blessing. The universe knew you could handle it and that, at your core, you are a perfect, abundant being who is capable of overcoming your issues with food and your body. I promise you that you haven't been given anything you can't handle.

You are wise, but the busyness of your mind has gotten the better of you. You've been overthinking, overanalyzing, and banging your head against a wall, trying to figure out how to just eat like a "normal person." Here's the thing: Brainpower will not break you out of this. You can't think your way out of your fight with food. You need to feel. You need to feel in order to heal.

When we are dieting, we run away from our bodies and take action out of fear. We hate how we look, so we jump on the next miracle diet in a desperate attempt to reach the ideal image we have of ourselves. Then, when we give up because we can't possibly sustain such restrictive routines filled with detailed meal plans and punishing exercise schedules, we tell ourselves we have no willpower and that we are failures at life. Sound about right?

It's time to revolutionize the way you release weight. Weight loss is an emotional issue and can't be sustained by restricting calories or spending a few more hours in the gym. The physical weight on your body is often a representation of the emotional weight you are carrying. We have to treat emotional problems with emotional solutions. We need to fully occupy our bodies and heal at our core so we are no longer victims to the madness in our minds.

This book will ease your frustration, speak to your struggle, and show you how to break free from your battle. I want you to get down and dirty when you implement the strategies I present in this book. Do the work and shift the emotional heaviness that is showing up on your heart and on your body. Then, and only then, will you be able to create sustainable transformation in your mind and body.

I've worked with hundreds of women in countries all over the world who are desperately looking for peace with food. Many of these women believed they had no chance in hell of ever loving their bodies or using food for health and hunger. I've spoken on stages around the world sharing my process of helping women break free of this cycle. I teach this process in my group programs and on my retreats, and now I get to share it with you in the pages of this book. I am so excited for you at the beginning of this journey. The unconditional self-love that you have been seeking is waiting for you just under the surface.

My philosophy is that weight loss needs to be a result of doing the emotional work, not the focus. My mission is to revolutionize the weight-loss industry by teaching women to dig into what they're actually hungry for, healing their emotional bodies first. When we are tuned into our bodies and listen, rather than numbing our emotions with food or punishing ourselves with restrictive diets and excessive exercise, we can use our awareness as a catalyst for growth.

We just have to remember that although pain is mandatory, suffering is optional. We prolong our suffering when we believe we don't have the ability to transform. We wait, we make excuses, and we self-sabotage. We beat ourselves up and throw obstacles in our way, which distance us from living our truth. Why? Because there is a small part of us that believes we don't deserve happiness.

But suffering is learned behavior, it's not innate within us. We are fundamentally designed to be happy. We are fundamentally designed to have light in our minds and in our bodies. Just like plants that lean into the sunlight to grow—you are designed just like that, to lean into the light. Trust me, love, you can begin to feel lighter in your body and your mind, and you can start right now.

I am telling you now, so make no mistake: You deserve happiness. I invite you to jump into this book with both feet. Come on a journey with me—a journey back into your body to reclaim your power and start loving yourself.

This is your chance, your turn, and I have your back through all of it. You've got this.

CHAPTER 1

WAKING UP TO YOUR TRUTH

My eyes felt sewn shut as I woke up in the hospital. I fought to lift my heavy lids, and the fluorescent brightness hit my eyes like a floodlight. The nurses moved in and out of the room; beeping noises from monitors connected to my body by wires made my head swim. I closed my eyes, then opened them again, and there was my boyfriend, Jake, sitting in a chair beside my bed. I was completely bewildered and then my head began to throb.

"Where am I? What happened?" I asked him, but my voice came out as a croak and I had to ask again. "Where am I?"

"Sam, you collapsed, and we had to rush you to the hospital."

I heard his words, but I couldn't make sense of it. I tried to piece it together. Where had I last been? But I didn't remember a thing. "Collapsed from what?" I stared at him, awaiting his response.

He looked at me almost afraid to tell me the answer. "Babe, you're malnourished." He said as he looked me in the eyes, "The doctors said you fainted because you haven't been eating enough." And then he looked down.

I blushed in a way that I immediately hoped Jake hadn't seen. And then I knew exactly why I was in that hospital bed—whether or not I was willing to tell myself the truth. Whether or not I was willing to admit to myself what was really going on, I knew that I was in that bed because my relationship with food was out of control.

It took only a split second to shift gears and hide my shame

I tried to look stunned and said, "You're kidding me." My priority was to hide my disordered eating, and I knew that if I could convince Jake it was a simple mistake, that would be all the easier. In that moment, my embarrassment trumped any meager worries I had about my health. It was far more important that no one know what I had begun to know was true.

Jake looked back up at me, forcing me to face the truth of my self-abuse. Nothing in my life up until that point had felt more painful. Staring into the eyes of someone I loved dearly and realizing he knew my deepest, darkest truth—that I was living in a constant state of extreme deprivation—was a waking nightmare. For just a second I knew he could see the lonely girl hiding behind the constant swirl of friends and partying. He could see I wasn't just depriving myself of food, but also of love, truth, and connection.

The only words I could muster were, "I'm sorry. I feel so bad."

I did feel terrible about having worried him, but I wasn't just apologizing for worrying him. I was apologizing for my existence, apologizing for my pain. I meant exactly what I said on so many levels. I felt so bad.

I was in Australia, over 8,000 miles from my home in Canada, trying to discover who I was and who I was going to be. And somehow in all of this process I had landed in the hospital for an ailment that was completely self-inflicted.

If I was honest, I wanted my mom. My mom has always been my best friend and right then she was very, very far away. And at the same time, I knew that everything about what was going on in that moment meant I couldn't tell her what was going on inside me.

The doctor came in and stood over my hospital bed, clipboard in hand. He gazed down at my face, at the tubes coming out of my nose, and said, "Ms. Skelly, you will need to consume at least 2,500 calories to restore your system and avoid relapse."

Relapse? I thought. That seemed more than a little dramatic. *I'm only dieting, why are you treating me like an addict?*

The truth about my behavior and the repercussions of my obsession with severe caloric restriction to manipulate my body were staring me right in the face, so I agreed to the doctor's orders. But the idea of consuming 2,500 calories was a suggestion that seemed ludicrous to me. I had been consuming less than 1,000 calories per day for the past eight months straight. I agreed outwardly, nodding, but inside I resisted.

The doctor looked at Jake and gave him a head nod, the kind of bro signal that communicates understanding without words. "She needs to stay here another night to complete the refeeding process, then you can take her home."

I had moved to Australia only eight months before that little trip to the hospital. I was fresh out of high school and desperate to escape the ordinary route that I saw all my friends beginning to take, the route other people wanted for me, but I really didn't want for myself. I didn't want to go to college, get a good-paying job, work my ass off, get married, and be all the things that were expected. I wanted something more, something unexpected. And while landing in the hospital for malnutrition was unexpected, this wasn't what I had in mind. I was in Australia looking for adventure, looking to find who I might be beyond what everyone expected. I had failed to look at who I was beyond my weight. I believed everything our culture said about the importance of the number on the scale and what that number "should" be. I had come to believe that my entire worth was dependent upon what I believed my body "should" be.

So how did I get here? Well, not long after landing in my adventure, I found myself on a beach, in a bikini. And I noticed that my body didn't exactly look like I wanted it to.

What I thought I saw as noticeable stomach rolls may honestly have just been the skin on my belly folding around my book. But I felt ashamed of my body all the same. I grabbed my outer thigh and made cellulite surface and chastised myself. And I had the thought, *You're getting fat, this is disgusting. You are worthless.* I thought these things, I believed myself, and then I worked hard not to feel anything at all.

Thoughts like these probably sound familiar to anyone who has ever struggled with their weight and/or their relationship with food. These types of thoughts work to tear you away from who you are and toward who you think you "should" be. It doesn't really matter who you are or what kind of family you grew up with, it is incredibly easy to get caught up in this inner demand to appear or actually be perfect.

I listened as my inner critic narrated my experience—and she was relentless. The ongoing narration of my deepest fears and vulnerabilities on constant loudspeaker caused me to shrink into a version of myself I was afraid to show the world. I hid behind my mask of perfection. I hid behind wit and charm. I did my very best to look perfectly put together on the outside—with makeup and hair done, trendy clothes, and a bright smile on my face—and I tried hard not to show anyone how terrified I really was or what I really thought about myself. My fight with food and my body was all-consuming. I let caloric intake determine my strength, and my weight determined my worth.

Honestly, I think control over my food and my body gave me a false perception of safety. Moving to Australia just ramped up my need for safety, and my need to control things got really, really out of control. The more I had to control, the less I could trust myself or anyone else's perception of me.

So by the time I landed in the hospital eight months later, I really didn't trust myself to eat for health and hunger. I had been calculating and planning every calorie I consumed for so long that I had completely forgotten what it even felt like to respond to my body's signals or cravings. It was as if that time in my life before was deleted and forever forgotten. I was so deep in my shame cycle, deep in my disconnection. I was so deep in my "shit" that I had no idea how to even breathe, let alone eat properly.

✦ ✦ ✦

The doctors agreed to let me go, I assured them I would be on my best behavior, and as soon as I was home my phone lit up with a text from my mom. "Jake said you've been in the hospital. Call home now!" I panicked, and part of me wanted to text Jake to shut his big mouth, but instead I sucked it up and called Mom.

"Honey, what's wrong? What happened?" My mom's words were a worried rush.

My heart felt heavy as the lie left my mouth. "It's all good, Mom. I was just trying to save money here in Australia and didn't want to waste it on food."

Mom paused, and the silence killed me. "For God's sake, Samantha, smarten up!" This was her classic line—whenever I was being a special kind of idiot, like this. The heartache of lying to Mom and minimizing the seriousness of what I had just done to myself made me feel sick to my stomach, but the fear of her knowing the truth—seeing what Jake had seen—felt worse.

For many people, landing in the hospital would be enough to wake up to the truth of what they were hiding, but for me it wasn't quite that simple. Just days after coming home from the hospital, I was caught up in my old cycle. I tethered myself to the electronic calorie-counting leash I'd adopted eight months before. I entered everything, and if I exceeded 1,000 calories, I would do jumping jacks and sit-ups until I burned it all off. I never considered myself to be a mathlete, but I sure was committed to this constant daily practice of adding and subtracting.

After we'd been dating for several months in Australia, Jake needed to go home to London for work. And we were moving to London together. We'd met in Australia, and what had begun initially as an impulsive first date after a shift at the bar where we both worked had become more. I thought this was the beginning of my real life, my off-the-beaten-path, I-made-it-all-up-myself life. With Jake. I told my mom I had found The One, fielded all her questions about when I would return to Canada to settle down, and felt her disappointment in learning that it wouldn't be for a few more years yet.

This is how I found myself running an upscale London salon, with a terrible boss, a crumbling romantic relationship, and an even worse relationship with myself, my food, and my body. Funny how difficult it can be to continue to be in love with someone else when you don't love yourself. And after just a few years, I was feeling entirely drained by the whole thing.

Jake, the one I fell madly in love with and moved across the world for? Somehow, we had fallen completely out of love, and the thought of having sex with him made me ill. But the thought of addressing the change in our relationship scared me. I feared the truth, and I feared the upheaval the truth would bring if I told Jake it was over. So I stayed with him, miserable and paralyzed by my fear of change.

More than resenting my sexless relationship, I resented my job. I managed the most prestigious hair salon in London. I was responsible for managing 40 hairdressers on my own. Actually, by "managing them" I mean that I was the dumping ground for their emotional tantrums and shit fits. It was a hostile environment where they thought being creative translated to lacking any personal accountability and projecting their emotions onto me.

The truth was I missed myself, the person I believed I used to be. I missed the optimistic girl who was always in love with life and everyone around her. Here I was, halfway across the globe, in a job that was not anything I actually wanted to be doing, in a city that gave me constant anxiety, and, as I would later realize, in the unhappiest relationship of my life.

My boss was even worse. He was the annoying kind of posh English gentleman who gently sips old-fashioneds with his pinky raised, but is crass and embarrassing in private. He'd come into my office like a hurricane, smother me in anxiety, and then leave. He had installed a camera in my office, which played in the kitchen of his apartment upstairs from the salon. The thought of him watching me made me feel like a cam girl, and on top of everything else my undereating had come to include uncontrollable binges.

One day after one too many of my staff's problems landed on my plate and my boss put yet another task that didn't fit my job description in front of me, I decided I had to get out of there for the rest of the day. I slammed my office door, slung my bag over my shoulder, and headed for home. Meandering through the cobblestone streets of Marylebone, one of the most affluent parts of London, I caught the eyes of the British women wreaking of perfume and pumped full of Botox as I passed. I missed home. I missed the cheerful optimistic city of my birth, where people smiled and looked you in the eye. My life in London felt like it was coming apart at the seams.

As I walked up the steep steps of my flat, I grabbed the handrail as if I was pulling myself up. It felt like a walk of defeat. I reflected on who I used to be, the joy that would emerge from my being—being completely happy in my body for no reason, waking up, taking on the world without trying to be someone else. Where did she go? I wanted that version of myself back.

And so, I called the person I believed might know how to help me find her: my mom.

"Mom," I said, "I am, and I have been, really unhappy."

"Baby," she said, "it's time to come home."

The truth of my mother's words sunk into me like a stone. I knew she was right. I needed to go home. I needed to admit just how far from home I really was. And it was not just my home in Vancouver, British Columbia, where I had grown up. I had drifted so far from the person I knew myself to be. I was so far away from the home I needed to inhabit, my home inside my body. The feeling of being at home in my body had become completely foreign to me.

Living the lies I had created for myself about the relationship that I was pretending to be happy in, the facade of success in the job that I hated, and knowing how far out of alignment I was with my sense of self and my relationship to my body gave me a visceral feeling that brought me to the edge of nausea. Have you ever been in this place? Your body is screaming the answers to you, but you convince yourself and those around you that you're not sure what to do.

We lose our power when we avoid the truth. We lose our power when we walk around pretending that we are okay when really, we are uncomfortable, unhealthy, and unhappy. Admitting to yourself that you're in a deadlock with your inner bully can feel nearly impossible. But then committing to doing everything you can to get out of the problem you have come to see as completely overwhelming, well, that feels like an insurmountable amount of work.

The truth will set you free, yes, but it will first piss you off. There is no inconvenience that is too great. There is no amount of work, when it's for your highest good, that isn't worth it. In fact, every ounce of pain, shame, and embarrassment I endured on this path allowed me to move through layers that set me free, but I first needed to face the truth that at the same time was so incredibly inconvenient. I needed to face the fact that I'd been in an illusion, existing in a reality that was eating my soul alive, an illusion that kept me distanced from my highest self.

When we face the truth, we release anxiety. Anxiety is a function of not being in our truth; it's a sensation that gives us feedback to let us know that we are living in a reality that is harming our soul in some way. There will be times that will be uncomfortable. Maybe you'll even feel like throwing this book away because some of the truths I will invite you to look into are often going to be uncomfortable. Stay with me, love. I know we just met, but I got you.

We are on this journey together, I have been through the long journey, and you can go through it, too. We are connected in this. In general people share the same fears, the same doubts, the same feelings of unworthiness. We also share the ability to reach a state of bliss and love that the majority of the world doesn't realize they have access to.

That is my invitation to you. I invite you to face the truth in your own life. I invite you to see the lies you have been telling yourself. You are invited to release your stories around being stuck or having no willpower, as they are keeping you addicted to the illusion that there is something wrong with you that you can't fix.

I promise you, at the end of this journey, you can discover a lightness you've never felt, an ease around food, and a feeling of self-love that will make you feel alive. I've got you the whole time. Lean into the process, feel into the parts of yourself you've been at war with, and know that you are worthy of freedom.

This isn't a book you read, flip to the last page, then place on your bookshelf to collect dust. This isn't the kind of book that, when you get to the end, you say to yourself, "That was interesting," then do nothing about it. In order to make this book work for you, there is work to be done!

INTEGRATIVE PRACTICE

First things first: You are going to need a notebook or journal to work through the exercises in this book. If you do not yet have one, do not pass go, do not collect $200: Go directly to the nearest store and buy yourself a journal. ASAP. It doesn't have to cost much, and it doesn't have to be fancy. Just find one that is a place you will feel good about collecting your thoughts and experiences as you work through this journey. (That said, you can make it as fancy or expensive or silly or serious as you want; whatever makes you feel like it is specifically yours.) If you don't yet have a journal, resist the urge to move beyond this chapter before you get one.

Go on, I will wait. . . .

Okay, got your journal? Let's get started.

If you're here, reading these words, it's your time to end the cycle you have with your body and change your relationship to food. It's time to become all that you were designed to be. I don't believe in coincidences and I don't believe you are here reading this book by accident. This is a key part of your path and when you complete this book, there will be no going back to what was. You're not here on this earth simply to pay bills, diet, then die. You're here to create a masterpiece out of your life. Somewhere along the line, you got a little sidetracked, you followed the shiny balls that led you to believe untruths, and I'm here to bring you back home.

You are going to own your truth and decide your path, right here in this moment. Will you choose your power over your fear? Will this be your time to change your life? This book contains the tools you have been seeking to transform—to change from the inside out. I need you to come halfway, meet me here within these pages, and spend time with these exercises so you can really absorb everything that I have to teach you. My commitment to you is to hold the vision of what is possible, guiding you through with my words and all the ways I share the mission. All you need to do is show up and do the work.

Journaling: Start with the Truth

Have you ever heard the phrase, "The truth will set you free"? Well now is the time for some of that truth. In the first part of this practice, you are going to write down some truths that perhaps you have been avoiding, by answering the following questions in your journal:

1. Is there a truth about your body and your relationship with food that has been nagging at you to see, but you have ignored the signs?

2. Where were some opportunities for changing your relationship with yourself in your life that you may have missed?

3. What are some of the signs that this change you are seeking has been coming for a very long time?

You can freewrite and be creative with these exercises or you can use some of these sentence starters:

- One thing I love about myself is . . .

- One thing I love about my body is . . .

- One truth I want everyone to know about me is . . .

- One truth about myself I am afraid to admit is . . .

- One lie I have been telling myself is . . .

Journaling: Letter of Commitment

In the second part of this practice, you are going to write yourself a letter of commitment, a declaration. When you are finished, hang it in your bathroom to remind yourself of the commitment you've made. This is your future self, the one who no longer fights with food, the version of you who feels peace in your body, the version of you who is present to all of life.

Here are some sentence starters to jump-start your writing process for this second half of the exercises:

- I am committed to letting go of . . .

- After I finish this book, my relationship with food will be . . .

- After I finish this book, my relationship with my body will be . . .

- My commitment to myself is . . .

CHAPTER 2

EXITING THE DIET DEPRESSION

We often heal slowly, in small increments. Before I could arrive at the truth of who I had become and how to get to a place where I could begin to heal, I had to come to some realizations. And realizations take time. For instance, not long before I decided to move home I found myself in a restaurant with my boyfriend, Jake.

I glanced down at the menu, and my mind began to spin around calculations of the caloric intake of multiple items. I could feel the pit in my stomach, hoping to God Jake wouldn't notice or sense my anxiety.

"Whatcha getting, love?" he asked as I was trying to figure out how many steps on the StairMaster I'd have to complete in order to burn off the fettuccine Alfredo. I was so hungry I knew that if I ordered the pasta with cream sauce I wouldn't be able to stop eating it, I would eat until the huge plate was gone, and if I couldn't stop eating Jake would see me eating like a maniac and know something was up.

I looked up at him, eyes glazed and mind spinning as I tried to fumble my way through an answer I thought was appropriate. "Probably a salad."

Of course, I was going to get the salad. As if I could eat a plate of fettuccine smothered in Alfredo sauce without immediately berating myself for having no willpower. The waiter came over and asked to take my order.

"I'll get the house salad, no croutons, no cranberries, no cheese, no dressing," I said.

Jake looked up from his menu. "You eat like a rabbit."

I knew I was going to choke down this salad, still want more, but not allow myself to have it. I only had 340 more calories to consume to hit my goal caloric intake for the day, which, by the way, was a completely made-up number in the first place. I read in magazines that if you eat 500 calories less than the recommended caloric intake, you'll lose weight or maintain, so I followed it to a tee, and when I didn't, I'd punish myself in the gym. Restriction dictated my entire life. It consumed every thought and flooded every move I made. Everything revolved around restricting my caloric intake, and if I "messed up," or failed to meet my unhealthy restriction, the rest of my day would be spent berating myself.

I had already trained to become a personal trainer, so I knew for a fact that this wasn't healthy, and that was always the interesting thing about my eating disorder. I knew better, I just didn't do better. I couldn't logic my way out of it. The voice in my head told me I wasn't thin enough—and if I wasn't thin, I wouldn't be worthy of love or acceptance—and I believed it.

The morning after my sad salad dinner, the piercing screech of my alarm woke me with a shock. It was still dark. I shut off the alarm, chugged the large glass of water from my bedside table, and stopped by the kitchen to prep my coffee, before immediately heading to the bathroom to weigh myself.

This was my morning routine. Each morning I would weigh myself to track my progress, which was really just a system to understand how much I needed to shame myself that day in order to achieve a weight I deemed acceptable. After last night's dinner and the bathtub's worth of laxative tea I drank before bed, I assumed today's number would be one that didn't flood my body with shame.

I opened the bathroom door and touched the scale with my foot to turn it on, waiting for the "000" to appear on the digital screen, and then stepped on. Waiting for the numbers to appear created so much anxiety. I closed my eyes as I waited for the three numbers to flash and then I looked down at them. To my disgust, I hadn't lost any weight at all. I don't know how many times this happened that I would push myself to the edge only to discover I hadn't lost the amount of weight I wanted, or I was exactly the same weight as the week before.

My heart sank and my stomach felt sick. I got off the scale and slid down the wall of the bathroom, curled there with my head in my hands and a relentless weight in my chest. My breath was shallow. I looked at myself in the mirror and thought, *How can I restrict more or work out harder to meet my goals for this week?*

You know the feeling of utter defeat? The feeling that you don't have the power to find the light in the darkness? That morning was just an average day during the period I have come to refer to as my "diet depression." My understanding of my worth was dependent on one thing and one thing only—the number on the scale and whether it matched the arbitrary number I had in my head that meant "perfection." My entire existence was consumed by the amount of physical weight on my body, and the drive to get it lower, to arrive at my idea of perfection, was excruciating.

Do you see what I was doing to myself? As my mind spun out—making calculations, workout plans, and grocery lists—my body sunk deeper into sorrow. I was letting my mind torture my body, because I didn't trust my body. I didn't believe my body had anything useful to tell me. I believed the only way to get what I wanted was to restrict further, push harder, to torture my body more. I constantly failed to see the beauty in my life. I failed to appreciate the blessings. And I was at a breaking point.

In the middle of my morning despair cycle, my watch beeped and I was suddenly aware that it was 6:55 and I was going to be late. "Shit," I said to my reflection in the mirror. "Now I'm going to be late." I wiped the tears out of my eyes, ran to the kitchen, grabbed my coffee, laced up my running shoes, and briskly walked to the park near my home to meet Hannah for her 7 A.M. personal training session.

I watched the steam create clouds above my coffee cup, the anxiety from the disappointment amplified as I began to spin myself into a further state of self-betrayal. I wondered what it would take for me to learn how to use food for health and hunger and not be disgusted with my body.

When I got to the park to meet Hannah for our workout, I saw her stretching by a tree and ran over to her and gave her a hug. But there was something in her eyes that told me she just wasn't feeling up to training, so I asked, "You all good, girl?"

As soon as I asked the question, her eyes welled up and her body drooped. "I can't handle my relationship with food! It's taking over my life," she confessed.

I was stunned. I felt like Hannah had read my mind. She was speaking the words to me that I so desperately wanted to speak to the world.

"It's taking over my life. It's all I think about and worry about," Hannah continued. "I feel this constant shame that takes over my body. I hate looking in mirrors and the thought of what I should eat and what I shouldn't spins me into the most intense anxiety!"

Her desperation was written across her face. I put my hand on my heart and nodded, holding space for her as she kept going.

"I've never told anyone this before. I have been hiding this pain from the world. I can't believe I'm telling you!"

I nodded. "How about we take a walk instead of a workout? I am not your trainer today, I'm your friend."

As we walked, I tried to build up the courage to share with Hannah my truth, my deepest truth around my struggle with food. I wished I had the words to tell her that I was struggling, too. That I was also at war. Instead I moved in and hugged her. I could feel her tears drop on my shoulder. In that moment, I felt so much compassion for her. I felt her pain, and I felt my pain, which was the same as hers. In that moment, I realized that she was going through the exact same thing that I was going through, and I knew that she needed to see she wasn't alone, so I stepped up. I took a deep breath, closed my eyes, and told her.

"I am struggling, too. Each day I fight this same battle," I finally admitted. "I can't believe I'm telling you this but pretending to be this beacon of light and love is killing me."

And then she did the most amazing thing, the most mundane thing, really—she smiled at me through her tears. I could feel a new lightness take over my body, and my fear of naming my truth subside. I could feel the pain of the whole morning shift as I connected with Hannah and admitted the truth.

"I can't believe I just told you that," I said to her as I giggled.

Hannah looked me in the eyes. "I thought you had your shit together. I would have never guessed that in a million years you were just as messed up as I am."

We both laughed at the insanity of what we had both thought a shameful secret. As we walked I felt relieved, connected, and for the first time in a long time, I felt like I was not alone. I realized that through my dieting I was isolating myself from anyone who might understand what I was going through. I had been unintentionally restricting my ability to connect to other people. By lying to myself and to everyone else about what I was doing to myself, and the toll it took on my physical and emotional health, I was essentially denying myself the love I thought I would gain if I reached my goal body weight.

Here's the thing about food restriction: You think you are just restricting your food, but you are actually restricting every relationship in your life. The intensity of the food restriction seeps into everything. It perpetuates this feeling, this message in your brain that there isn't enough, you can't have enough, and you are not enough. I restricted the love that I could receive, the connection and intimacy that is possible only when you are being generous with yourself, sharing your fears and vulnerabilities with others. I'd purposefully avoided deepening relationships because I was terrified that if people were too close they would realize that I wasn't healthy and that I was in a battle with food and they would see behind the facade that I had my shit together to the embarrassing truth of my diet depression. So I kept it on lock and shared just enough of myself to keep people from asking questions.

The way I was restricting myself was distancing me from the magic of life. I didn't allow myself to relish in the beauty of the everyday and savor the simple moments of joy because my mind was too consumed with the constant struggle. How could I enjoy simple moments when I insisted on focusing all my energy on my failures? On fixing the number on the scale? On counting every calorie? The only times I allowed myself to savor moments and relish in contentment was when my weight was deemed acceptable to the bully in my head.

The inconsistency between how we feel internally and how we are showing up externally is one of the most painful human experiences. The feeling that we need to wear a mask or that we need to prove something—seeking validation for our delusions from others—is exhausting. All I wanted was to show the world who I was, every part of me, but I was terrified of my dark and flawed truth. I was terrified of being unlovable and judged, so I remained imprisoned within the confines of my own mind, battling with myself and my emotions. My weapon of choice: food.

I did everything that would supposedly lead to change on the outside, assuming that change on the inside would follow. I read diet books with smiling women and perfectly toned tummies on the cover, testing out any plan I could find that promised results. I decided that if I had the perfect body and hit that magic goal-weight number, I would finally achieve the feeling of being loved that I craved. In my search for the answer to all this struggling and pain that I felt deep inside, I suppressed that inner voice and turned outward toward external ideals of beauty and acceptance, comparing my body to photos of models and actresses in magazines. I actually believed that if I hit my goal weight, everything in my life would slide into place. Of course, I was wrong. Nothing is further from the truth. By seeking validation solely from a number on a scale, I was denying my innate value and worth and driving every kind of satisfying love away, including self-love. And as if that wasn't punishment enough, I was punishing my body as well.

You are inherently worthy right in this moment. There is nothing you need to do, be, or change about yourself that impacts your worth. You are already completely worthy. You are already enough. You have inherent worth, in abundance, right in this very moment. Even if you can't feel it right now, even if you've never known it before. It is always there no matter what you do or how much you weigh; your worth is unconditional. It can't be altered or broken, and it's always present.

Recognizing and respecting your worth might take work—it certainly did for me—but that is the work we are here to do. It might require a little bit of separation from the outside world, the world of magazine covers and people on TV. Knowing your worth requires a connection between your mind and your body.

In order to truly attain physical health, you have to pay attention to mental health. We simply can't have one without the other. Dieters are often unaware of their mind-body connection because their mind and body feel at odds with one another. But make no mistake, your mental health is affecting your physical health and your physical health is affecting your mental health right now whether you are aware of it or not. It is completely possible to look healthy while doing some serious damage internally, because these aspects of our health are inextricably connected.

During my diet depression, I looked like the image of health from the outside, but on the inside I was deeply unhappy. Those around me labeled me as committed, dedicated, and hardworking, and these things were true. However, I was committed to the wrong things. I was dedicated to an aesthetic ideal, working hard for some outside notion of what I should be. I was not paying any attention to my health as a whole.

Everything I did was driven by the idea of my aesthetically perfect self, always just out of reach. And because of this my mental health was taking a hit. Each day I was taking my mental health and pushing it aside. *I'll deal with my emotions when I hit my goal weight,* I'd say to myself as I would enter every last calorie into my calorie-counting app before I went to bed. I neglected listening to what my body was saying, which kept me emotionally spun out and stuck in the never-ending cycle.

Here is what the other side of the diet pendulum looks like. I remember sitting on the kitchen counter of my flat in London on a Saturday midafternoon, trains going by outside of my window, still in my pajamas after a ridiculously difficult week at the salon where I was paid to look like I had it all together. There I was scraping the last of the Nutella from the bottom of the glass jar. I could feel my stomach cramping as I continued to put spoonful after spoonful into my mouth, telling myself with each scoop, *Just one more.* I knew what I was doing, and I knew it wasn't good, but I couldn't stop.

Thinking back at myself sitting on the counter with the jar of Nutella is a little like watching a thriller, you know the scene: The woman is about to enter the room where she definitely should not go, so you yell at the TV, "Nooo! Get away! Don't go in there, that is totally where the killer is!" I felt like my life was a series of these moments. Even while I was living them it was a little like I was the character and the watcher. In those moments I knew I should do better—I wanted to do better—but with no access to the tools I needed to see what was at the heart of my battle, I made bad choices. I walked into the wrong room again and again, cue the dramatic music.

I immersed myself in self-destructive behavior—overeating, then berating myself, denying my inner worth, practically starving myself to "make up for it." And as if that wasn't enough, then I would exercise to the point of exhaustion, ignoring signs of muscle strain and potential injury—I was a personal trainer and I knew the signs! My life was composed of consistent segments of depravation and overindulgence. There was absolutely no balance. I swung wildly from one side of the pendulum to the next.

As it turns out, there are very good scientific reasons for why one thing leads to another: I was fighting my own biology. By depriving myself constantly, I was unknowingly signaling to my body that food was a scarce commodity, so on the occasions when I allowed myself sugar or fat or carbs, my body would freak out—jumping on the opportunity to fuel up—and I would binge. I know that it sounds nutty, but my body basically would command me to overeat to the point of feeling sick. My starving system was just reacting naturally and overeating to compensate for the deprivation—it had no clue when I would feed it again so it had to get while the getting was good.

It was only at the bottom of the jar that I found the despair I had been running from with each spoonful. I could either look for another fix—a bag of chips, a chocolate bar—or start back in on the other side of punishment with crazy workouts, laxative teas, restricting my calories to a number fit for a mouse. I want to be able to tell you that I had a major realization in this particular moment holding that empty Nutella jar in my pajamas and that I reached for the phone to call someone who might understand what I was going through instead of a glass of wine. But the truth is that I wasn't ready to face my truth in that moment. I wasn't ready to ask my body what it needed from me and I wasn't ready to listen to the answers. So on this particular occasion I did not ask for help, I chose to numb out even further. I poured myself a glass of wine, drank it as fast as I could, and went to the couch to watch TV. I had two choices: 1. I could continue to abuse my mind and body with this cycle; or 2. I could look for the self-love that was already inside me. I chose the former—the harder route—because it was familiar. Facing what I was doing in the long term was too overwhelming, so I continued to numb myself.

When we consider what mind-set we are in when we engage in this kind of behavior we realize that both sides of the restriction-overeating pendulum are rooted in fear. When we restrict and undernourish ourselves, we ignore the body's natural wisdom. Because of our fear of gaining weight and lack of trust in the body's intuition, we create scarcity. Overeating is a natural response to that scarcity and deprivation.

After we have abused it and denied it, the body is fearful it will not be properly fed and so when food is made available, that's when the "I can't stop myself" binge happens and the body takes over the mind. You know when you're full but for some reason, instead of throwing the rest of it in the garbage or the doggie bag, you continue to put the food in your mouth? Pushing our bodies to this point—full to bursting—is violent and self-destructive. Overeating can feel like a punishment; it's like treating your body like a trash can or a take-out container, something that is disposable and unwanted.

Choosing to use food as a drug to numb our emotions is a fear-based decision just as hating the fat on our bodies and jumping on a restrictive diet is rooted in fear. So whether we are restricting or overeating, both actions are fear based. We can't break the cycle when we are operating from a fear-based mentality. We need to have acceptance in order to have sustainable transformation.

We've been conditioned to believe if we want to have change in our lives, it has to be hard—that we need to shame our way there—and this is what I have come to think of as "hating our way to happiness." It is a fundamentally broken model. When you picked up this book because you want to heal your relationship to food, your body, and yourself through kindness, love, and compassion, you rejected that old mind-set.

Trust me when I say that once you are practiced at it, viewing yourself with compassion instead of criticism is a hundred times easier and so much more enjoyable. However, it will require the part of you that wants to control everything and force your way through life to calm down, surrender, and relax, which I know can be a daunting task. That inner body-hating critic can be a real bully, and it can be hard to stand up to a bully.

Albert Einstein once said, "We cannot solve our problems with the same thinking we used when we created them." Therefore, if fear created the battle, we need a different mind-set to heal it. Bear with me during this process: There will be a part of you that will fight it, the part of you that thinks life needs to be hard for it to be worthwhile. Allow that part of you to relax and lean into gentle understanding and to trust with your whole self. You aren't alone in this, I've got you.

You have an infinite love inside you already, love beyond measure—it's time to start actively looking for it, listening for it, and feeling for it.

INTEGRATIVE PRACTICE

Right now, we are going to start practicing connection. Our bodies—our infinitely wise bodies—have all kinds of information that they are willing to share with us if only we listen to them. As we move through these chapters, we will begin exercises that practice the work of listening and feeling for the body's wisdom. We will call these exercises body scanning and body tasking. Ready? Let's get started.

Meditation: Body Scanning

For this exercise, I want you to find a quiet space and about 15–20 minutes of your day. Pick a time and place where you won't be interrupted. I know that this can be a difficult task, so you might want to put it on your calendar. Tell everyone you are unavailable and then close the door to your office or bedroom or any place that might allow you a little bit of quiet alone time.

Find a seat on the floor or in a chair and get quiet. If you are in a chair, place both feet on the floor and feel the ground beneath you. If you are sitting on the floor or lying down, feel where your body meets the ground. I want you to go inside your body now and just ask it how it feels. Start with your toes and work your way up through your legs, through your hips, pelvis, belly, and into your abdomen. Ask your shoulders and neck how they are doing, check in on your arms and hands. Feel your face and head. If you notice pain or discomfort in any part of your body, quietly take note without assigning any kind of judgment—positive or negative—to that discomfort.

Now that you have spent a little time connecting to your body and asking how it is doing—like you would with any old friend or cherished family member—I want you to ask your body a little bit about what it wants for itself. This might take a bit of an icebreaker because, if you are anything like I was, it may have been a minute since you really listened to what your body had to say. Begin by exploring some positive emotions to discover your body's reaction to them. Let's start with joy.

Imagine a time you felt joyful and happy, any time throughout your life that you felt really good. Stay right with that moment; don't move forward or backward from that time, just stay with that singular moment of joy. Imagine what that emotion felt like and bring that memory right into your body. What did each part of your body feel like? What was your posture like? How did your chest and shoulders feel? How did your spine and neck feel? How did you hold your head?

Next, think about confidence. I want you to remember the feeling you had when you last had the thought: *I got this; this right here is what I am good at.* In this process, negative thoughts may arise and that's okay. You can simply acknowledge any thoughts that do not serve your purpose and go back to your intention, which is to remember what confidence feels like. Simply tell those negative thoughts hello, but quietly remind them that right now your job is to remember how confidence feels in your body, and it is for a very good reason. You simply do not have time to engage your negative thoughts in a discussion because right now you are busy. Now you can really put yourself into your memory of confidence. What posture did your body assume? How did you hold your head, neck, and shoulders? How did your chest feel?

Then I want you to remember what being at peace feels like. Go through the whole entire exercise. Bring to mind a scene when you felt peaceful. How did that feel in your body?

Finally, I want you to imagine the future—that you have finished this book and you are at the end of this journey. In this future, you have ceased to cycle through restricting or overeating, and you and your body have come to really get along. You and your body have become very good friends. You aren't punishing your body and your body isn't punishing you. Do another body scan, starting with your toes and moving all the way up through the top of your head. Imagine that you have reached the end of this book and your relationship with your body is completely healed. What does that feel like inside your body from your toes on up? How does your posture change? How does this feel in your chest and neck? What thoughts come up?

Now it's time to journal about these things. What was this experience like for you? How did the different body scans feel? How did each emotion differ in your body? How did the different memories feel in your body? What were any thoughts that arose as you did these exercises?

Meditation: Body Tasking

With our first exercise we noted that our bodies have all kinds of information. Once you have begun to get used to checking in with your body—about how things feel, where different emotions reside, and how they feel in your body—we can begin digging deeper into more specific questions and issues. We will call this practice body tasking. In body tasking we are engaging in a conversation with our bodies to learn more about how we are feeling about something. Throughout this book we will come back to this practice but, to begin, let's use body tasking to find some support in your healing journey.

Begin with a conversation with your body about how you might find an understanding, supportive friend or confidante who could help you in your journey toward healing your relationship with your body and with food. Whether someone from your community, family, friends, co-workers—this person must be someone you can envision having an honest conversation with about these things. This might seem at the outset like a daunting task—after all, you have likely spent a lot of time and energy hiding these struggles from others in the past—so we will give the task to our intelligent and intuitive bodies.

Find a quiet place to think and 10–15 minutes to perform this exercise.

Start by brainstorming a list of potential people in your life who might make a good ally for your healing journey. Someone who might understand or just listen well. Has anyone you know talked to you about struggles with diet or weight?

Once you have made your list, sit in a chair with your feet on the ground and do a body scan to check in and say hello to your body. Start with your feet and move through your whole body, noting any areas of comfort or discomfort without judgment. If a negative thought or critical voice comes up, quietly acknowledge it and continue on with your task.

Once you feel you have connected with each part of your body, start to think of the first person on your list. Imagine the conversation you might have with this person about food issues. What does your body tell you in terms of how you might feel in this situation? There might be some nervousness at first; note what nervousness feels like and see if there are any other feelings that come up in your body. Does imagining what you might say to this person cause your body to straighten your spine, relax your shoulders, tilt your chin up? Does this imagined conversation cause you to tense up your neck and shoulders or concave your chest? Does the feeling resemble comfort or discomfort?

Moving through your list, what does your body's reaction to each person say to you? Write a quick note in your journal about each name and how your body has reacted to connecting with this person. What did your posture do? Did you feel butterflies in your stomach or some other part of your body? Did you get a sense of ease? Does that bodily reaction resemble peace, confidence, or joy? How about discomfort? After noting, move on to the next name on your list and repeat these steps.

If you come to the end of your list and you feel like things are not any clearer, give yourself a break. Not everything comes all at once. Take a break from this exercise and try again in a day or two.

If you came away from this experience with one or more names that feel like a good person to talk to about this process, you might give yourself a break anyway. Just a night's sleep is sometimes enough to give you more clarity or confidence before reaching out to see if a friend or family member has time to grab coffee and have a conversation.

If you do this exercise more than once and really no one in your community comes up as someone who might be a support to you or someone you can talk to occasionally about your healing journey, write a little entry in your journal about what you might want in a friend or confidante. Imagine what it might be like to have someone who would be understanding and supportive as you move through each exercise. I want you to set the intention for yourself to just keep an eye open for a person you could talk to and trust somewhere along the way. With your intention set, that this person will pop into your life, just as Hannah popped up for me on that day in the park.

CHAPTER 3

NO PAIN, NO GAIN

I met and fell in love with Jake almost as soon as I was settled in Australia. I was 18 years old, working in a club, and I felt like I was really making it on my own. Of course, all I was doing was working a shitty bar job with Aussies yelling drink orders at the top of their lungs. It was a hellish job, but it was *my* hellish job, so for a while I loved it.

One night, I started to close out at the end of my shift, my ears ringing from the loud music and patrons shouting to be heard over the loud music. I grabbed my cash bag and my gin and tonic with lime and headed to the back room to prepare to head home for the night. I pushed the swinging door open with my hip and noticed a man sitting at the far end of the long table in the middle of the room, and I did a double take.

"Hey," I said, sitting down at the other end of the table. "Are you new here?"

"Nah, I just work in the back. I've seen you around here and there."

His British accent made me straighten up in my chair a little, and his blue eyes made me curious about him. "So, what are you doing tonight?" he asked me, completely serious.

I motioned as if I was checking my watch. "Tonight? It's two in the morning."

"Yeah, it's prime time. Let's grab a drink."

My mind said no, but my mouth disagreed. "That sounds awesome. Let's do it!" I finished cashing out and threw my tips in my bag.

"Oh, by the way, I'm Jake." He threw out his hand and stared at me, not breaking eye contact. I could feel the confidence radiating off of him.

Isn't it strange how some of the most exciting and beautiful experiences of our lives can later become some of the most painful? The things that were so exciting at the beginning of a relationship can then become the very things that make it impossible to continue being in that relationship. Beginnings are lovely and easy. Endings, not so much.

The end of that relationship came five years later. We had moved to London, and I had come to resent a lot of what drew us together in the first place. We'd been living together for a year, and Jake's "2 A.M. is prime time to grab a drink" habit had slowly become a lot less fun. What I had thought was us being young and spontaneous had become Jake going out with his buddies until all hours of the night. Slowly I realized it was beginning to look a lot like substance abuse.

One night, Jake came home clearly on something. I thought, *Wow, I just don't want to do this forever. No matter what I thought before, no matter of my plans for the future, I just don't want to do this anymore.*

It was something like a moment of clarity.

When Jake woke up the next morning, I brought him a cup of coffee and looked at him through the steam rising from the cup. I screwed up all the courage I had and I said to him, "Jake. Listen. I think we could be really good together, but I just don't want drug use in my life. And if that is how you are going to live your life, I don't want to be in a relationship with you anymore."

It sounds so brave and clear as I write this, but it was so hard to say to him. All my fear of not being lovable surfaced, and I suddenly felt terrified that I was making a huge mistake in even daring to tell him we might break up. But there—I had told him. I had faced the truth and said it aloud and he had to cope with it.

And then Jake started to cry.

"You're right, babe. These nights have been getting out of control. I will stop, I won't do it anymore."

This should have made me feel better. It was the best of both worlds, right? I could stay with Jake and not have to put up with his substance abuse. It should have made me feel elated. And at first, I did feel relieved but, somehow, I also felt a little disappointed. But I pushed that disappointment down, as I did with most of my negative feelings then. Now I know where that disappointment came from. It came from the part of me that knew Jake wasn't right for me, drug use or no. Jake was a distraction.

For me, and in the mind of many dieters, anything to ease our obsessive thoughts about food and body can be attractive. Anything to distract the inner critic that always feels like she's on loudspeaker is a win. Focusing on "fixing" my relationship was a fantastic distraction from my inner critic. If I was more honest with myself, I might have admitted that my whole relationship with Jake had become untenable. It wasn't just the drinking and drug use. I was looking for a way to concentrate on anything but myself and my issues with food, so I poured all of my mental energy into a failing relationship.

Why did I do that? Well, suffering had begun to feel comfortable after a while. You know those hugs, the ones you get from an overly excited hugger, where for a split second you feel like you're suffocating, but you stay still and bear the hug anyway? It felt exactly like that, only it lasted a hell of a lot longer. Think every day, for months. I was allowing myself to be suffocated, convinced that—like the overly excited hugger—Jake meant well and didn't realize he was hurting me. I endured the pain and struggled—martyring myself to be the good, supportive girlfriend I was "supposed" to be. It became part of my identity, so much so that I was addicted to it. The struggle fed me. It was poison, but I had convinced myself it was medicine.

Each day I fought with myself trying to "figure it out" and "figure him out." The entire relationship was emotionally exhausting, and I stayed with him way longer than I wanted to. And the whole time I justified it by telling myself that I needed to learn a lesson and the pain was evidence that I was growing.

We've been conditioned to think that things have to be hard for them to be worthwhile, and if something is painful, it means we are growing. But there was no shiny gift on the other side of this—no perfect boyfriend who skipped nights partying with the boys to hang with me, his healthy, happy girlfriend who ate only when she was hungry and didn't judge her worth by numbers on the scale. Day after day, I convinced myself that if I could just be a better girlfriend, then it would all be great. I told myself that one day I would be good enough, he would change, and then poof: I would feel better in my relationship.

I was terrified to admit that Jake and I were wrong for each other. It went against the fantasy I had created in my mind of the life we would have together. I never told him any of this, mind you. I not only needed to break up with

Jake, I needed to break up with the fantasy and get real with myself.

After that conversation, Jake cleaned up his act—for a couple of weeks, anyway. He kept his word and slowed down the partying to a reasonable pace. And then one night he did not come home at all. He rolled into our apartment at 8 A.M., flopped on the bed, and passed out. I had been up most of the night worrying.

I found drugs in his wallet. I shook him awake, threw the little baggie in his face, and said, "I hope it was worth it."

For once, I saw my moment and I took it. I could so easily have given in to another round of suffering as a distraction—but I didn't. I gave myself permission to take the out he had offered me, packed up my things, and moved out.

I was finally done with that relationship. But that meant I had nothing to focus on but myself, my body, and my relationship to food. So of course, I hopped right in to dieting my way into a whole new me.

It's so easy to get caught up in this illusion that if something is hard, it must be good for us, not just in relationships, but in every aspect of our lives. What doesn't kill you makes you stronger, right? No pain, no gain? What I've learned is that there's a fundamental difference between emotional pain and emotional suffering. Emotional pain is necessary; it is the way we learn and grow. We cannot grow by avoiding the pain and ignoring the darkness. But emotional suffering is something else entirely, and it serves no purpose whatsoever. Suffering doesn't make us stronger or better, it just drags our pain out over months and years.

Pain is how you know something is out of alignment (the immediate, sharp pain of a broken bone), but suffering happens when you make the choice not to take steps to alleviate the pain—allowing the bone to heal without having it set properly so that it aches for the rest of your life. Emotional pain is momentary and it's often a sensation we feel in our bodies like physical pain. Now, if you aren't connected to your body, then it can be difficult to experience or interpret the physical sensations of emotional pain. I have spent much of my life disconnected from my body, so I understand.

But it does happen. Think about when someone says they have "butterflies" in their stomach. What does that mean they are feeling emotionally? You know immediately they are nervous—we've all felt that. When someone says that they are "heartbroken" or even "in love" they often physically press on their chest to emphasize where they feel the emotion they are experiencing. These statements are not just random phrases, but evidence that we as humans universally tap into our body's intuition, experiencing a physical sensation and location in the body for each emotional state. When we are aware of our bodies and listening closely, we can feel our emotions physically and use sensation as a guide. Emotional pain, like any other kind of pain, has a physical home in the body.

It is reasonable to think: *I am in pain, therefore something is out of whack and I need to correct it or heal from it.* But it is completely unreasonable to think: *I am in pain, therefore I am fundamentally flawed and I will always feel this way.*

When we are in pain, the best thing we can possibly do is to feel it and ask it what it needs from us. "How can

I help you?" or "How can I love you?" are two powerful questions we can ask when we are in pain. Pain is simply data. It's a beautiful indicator that something is not quite right. But we easily turn pain into suffering when we ignore it, suppress it, justify it, or numb it.

When we numb this divine data with food, drugs, alcohol, or anything else we might use to distract us from our emotions, we simply can't learn from our pain. We can't extract the lessons from it, so we stay stuck, and the pain is then shifted into suffering. And suffering quickly becomes stagnant in the body. Suffering leads to false beliefs about who we are and how we operate in the world. It becomes a worldview that we wake up with in the morning and go to bed with at night. It's everlasting. Eventually we just decide that "that's just how we are," and we live with it, so numbed that we are unaware that every single moment of it is completely unnecessary and self-imposed.

I stayed in my relationship with Jake for so long because it felt easier to change nothing than to face the painful truth of a breakup—and so I suffered through a relationship that just didn't fit me anymore. It is avoiding the pain that makes suffering occur.

Ultimately, we need to completely change the relationship we have to our emotional pain. In our culture, most people avoid pain at all costs—bottling it up to "grin and bear it." The problem with our relationship to pain as it stands and purely avoiding it is that in doing so we fail to learn from it and heal it before it becomes suffering. In order to change our relationship to emotional pain we have to be able to recognize it as our truth, accept it, and take action to heal it.

The good old saying "the truth hurts" is accurate. Facing the truth of what is, when you are attached to how it *should* be, is a painful realization. It's painful to look at yourself in the mirror and drop all the masks—the shame and the doubt—and admit you've been living in terror within your own body. It's painful to admit that you have lost all hope and feel like you're dying inside. It's painful to be met with the truth. The truth may hurt for a period of time, but the ongoing suffering of dishonesty toward yourself is a far greater burden to carry.

We need to change the way we interact with not just the physical sensation, but also with our stories surrounding emotional pain. And that means we need to locate the sensations of emotional pain within the mind as well as the body. We develop negative associations with pain because we have been conditioned to from a young age. Think about yourself as a child: Can you recall a time when your pain—physical or emotional—was labeled as "bad"? Has anyone ever told you to "stop crying" or "toughen up"? Of course, these words from our parents or caregivers aren't intentionally destructive; however, they cause us to process our pain as "wrong" and can cause us to spend our entire lives burying that pain, hiding it from ourselves and others. When, in reality, the best thing we can do is simply allow these emotions to process and feel them fully.

It's vital to get clear on your story around the sensations of pain that you experience in your body. We have strong associations to the feelings in our systems. As soon as we feel a sensation in the body, we immediately attach a meaning to it—just like we were taught as children. If you were told to "toughen up" when you cried, you may have internalized a narrative that sadness and pain are wrong and weak. But the truth is, there is no meaning. Sensations in the body are neutral, but the meaning we give them often causes us to spin out into suffering.

Think about the sensation of anxiety for a moment— that quickening pulse, that fight-or-flight instinct. Do you try to tamp it down or do you let it drive you into a frenzy? Think about the meaning you've given that feeling based on your past. What do you say to yourself when it arises? What actions do you want to take as soon as you feel it? What is the meaning you give it?

We are meaning-making machines. We can literally create meaning around anything in life, and that meaning can elevate us, or depress us completely. The same exact thing can happen to two completely different people, but if they create two completely different narratives, they will have two completely different meanings.

Let me give you an example: A woman in a red dress is walking through a busy restaurant on her way to meet her friend for dinner. As she passes by, a group of women at another table give her appraising looks up and down. The woman in the red dress notices this attention. There are two different stories she could create here: She might feel the women at that other table are judging her body, that her outfit looks horrendous, and that she would have been better off not leaving the house at all. Her strong association leaves her feeling awful, judged, and insecure.

Or, she could be filled with excitement, awe, and grati-tude that the women sitting at the table took the time out of their meal to notice her outfit, which was perfectly put together. This makes her feel admired. This is the exact same scenario, but in this case the woman leaves feeling alive, empowered, and full of confidence.

Without being aware of it, we all from time to time react like the woman in the first scenario. We unknowingly put ourselves in states of anxiety and depression because we are assigning negative meanings to situations that could be interpreted in a positive way.

Let's start with the pain you feel about your relationship with food: What meaning are you giving that pain in your life? When you feel it in your body, what is your instant reaction to the feeling? Take note of this as you're reading these words. How does your body feel? What does your posture look like? What associations do you have with this feeling? What associated cravings do you feel? Are these associated cravings a means of escape?

Now let's explore something for a moment. What if, as soon as you feel the physical markers of the emotional pain associated with food in your body, you chose a different meaning? What if the meaning you gave pain was empowering: a recognition of knowing this truth about yourself, a signal that you are awake to the issues in your life, and a revelation that change is possible? What if you decided each time you felt that particular pain that it meant you had an invitation to dive deeper into your body and learn something new about yourself? Self-knowledge is a powerful thing and even recognizing that your pain stems from a destructive relationship with food is a step toward healing.

When we approach pain from this vantage point, we allow our *hearts* to solve the misalignment, rather than our heads, and we open up the conversation to one of growth, rather than self-hate.

Nowadays, there is an element of my body that feels excitement when I am met with pain, because I have decided in advance that when I feel it, I am learning, I am growing, and I am expanding. There is an element of childlike curiosity that arises when I am feeling anxious.

What this does is it calms my nervous system down, it takes me out of being reactive and defensive, and I allow the part of my brain that is responsible for compassion to activate and help me navigate what I am feeling.

When we use food to numb this sensation, this signal from our body, we miss out on the lesson. We miss out on the opportunity to grow. Our resistance to feeling these sensations is likely what keeps us stuck in the cycle of bingeing and dieting. When we increase our capacity to feel, we release the need for food to numb those feelings. When we release the need for food to numb ourselves, weight loss becomes a result of doing the work, not the focus.

This work, this doing the real difficult work of facing what is actually making us overeat or undereat and then go back again? This is how we are going to ultimately change the face of the weight-loss industry that is keeping us overweight and overwhelmed. It's essential that we stop putting Band-Aids on bullet wounds and get to the core issue of why we feel stuck and at war with ourselves when it comes to our relationship to food and our bodies.

You, my love, are not only inside the body that is the home of all of these sensations, you are that body. The fleeting sensations of pain or joy that your body holds are just that—fleeting sensations felt by a body. They are not you, and you are not them. You are simply the body that holds it all. When you can recognize the difference between the sensations you feel and your true self, you will find states of freedom that you never knew were possible. This is the art of observation, and it allows us to be in a space where we can take full responsibility for our emotions. But remember, taking responsibility for your emotions is not the same as taking on those emotions as your identity. For example, if you feel sad and alone, instead of thinking, *I am sad. I am alone*, tweak your perspective slightly—rewrite your narrative—and think, *I am feeling sadness and disconnection. How can I heal this sensation?* As soon as we identify with our emotions—labeling ourselves—we keep ourselves stuck in a negative story with no ending. Instead of saying, *I am anxious*, change the story to, *I am experiencing bodily sensations and thoughts of anxiety.* Separating your essence and identity from your ever-changing sensations and emotions consciously by choosing the way you speak to yourself is a small change, but it will change everything.

At the core, all you are is light and love. At the very core, you are a being of wholeness. Remember you are so much greater than all your parts combined. You are infinite, wise, and powerful. It's time to rise up above your limitations and live in a place where love is abundant. It's available now and you're more than worthy.

This simple yet profound practice of learning from your body and separating who you are—your story and your worth—from your emotions will ultimately shift the way you relate to your pain. Pain is a beautiful teacher. It shows us exactly what we aren't seeing and what we aren't loving. It guides us to the parts of ourselves that need the deepest healing. Pain is the portal to our truth.

INTEGRATIVE PRACTICE

Meditation: Tapping into Pain

Right now, as you read this, locate where in your body you might be feeling a little tense or anxious. Allow yourself to relax your shoulders. Take a deep breath and feel into that place. What does it feel like? Notice the sensations. Don't judge them, just simply notice. When we shift our judgment of our sensations into pure curiosity with love, we can really observe them. We can begin to really look at them as they are, not as worse than they are. Allowing these sensations to just be there, and loving them fiercely, will allow us to transcend them in ways we didn't know were possible.

Notice your pain, observe it with love, and then ask, "What am I not seeing?" This question is beautiful, as it allows the body to guide the experience. It allows the body to show us what might be missing, what we are not seeing with our eyes and logical minds.

I always say, "I am so much smarter when I don't use my brain," and this is the absolute truth. When we surrender the mind and allow the wisdom of the body to take over, we get to live deeper in our truth. We get to release our busy mind, the part of us that obsesses, and allow our hearts to make decisions that are in alignment with our souls.

Tap into the pain, observe it with love, release the judgment, and notice how you feel. Notice the sensation—see if you can bring even more love to it, even more stillness, and even more patience. See what happens when you settle deeper into the feeling. Turn it up a little more as you allow your heart to open up even more.

It seems counterintuitive to want to "turn up the feeling" or intensify it, especially if you have spent most of your life denying or numbing these painful places within yourself. But in order to fully process the sensation and release it, you need to exhaust it. If you hold on to any part of it, it will simply come up again later—with a vengeance. Feel deeply and work through the entire sensation now, while it is manageable, not once it's gotten too confusing and painful to bear.

Breathe deeply into the feeling, in through the nose and out through the mouth. As you breathe, feel the feeling even more. You can put down the book for a moment as you do this. Breathe in and out. As you breathe, imagine white light is coming in through your nose, down into your body, and lighting up the part of you that feels tense, tender, or suppressed. Imagine that light illuminating your system from within, letting the light drench love all over this sensation. Then ask the question, *How can I love you more?* Notice how the body opens up even more.

Journaling: Rewrite Your Story

What are your stories around pain? When you experience the sensation that you identify as "pain," or maybe anxiety or depression, what is the meaning you assign it?

It's time to rewrite the stories you tell yourself and create new stories, stories that are conducive to your healing around food and your body. When we change the stories we have around pain—and ultimately change the entire relationship we have with pain—we can move through that sensation with more grace and ease, which allows our ego to settle, thus making the process of healing and transformation so much easier. It's time to make that shift. It's time to anchor in new stories that allow you to thrive. It's important that you anchor in and remind yourself of these new, empowering stories on a regular basis. Your brain will fight you on this, as those old stories are oddly comfortable, even though they create pain. Be patient and kind to yourself in this process, because it takes some time to untangle old narratives that no longer serve you. Self-compassion is not an option here, it's essential.

Okay, let's get started. You can freewrite and be creative with both of these exercises or you can answer a few of the questions below to start you off:

- What are your current stories around pain?

- How have these stories kept you in a state of suffering?

- What has it cost you to stay in this destructive pattern?

- What are the new stories you're going to create around pain?

- How will your actions and behaviors change when you now interact with pain?

- How will this massively benefit your transformation?

CHAPTER 4

PERFECT IS THE ENEMY OF GREAT

Nearly a year after leaving Jake and leaving London, I entered a fitness competition back in Canada. I spent months training, thinking that this was the way to a healthy relationship with my body. If I could prove to everyone else I was fit, if I could dedicate all of my time to it, then this would become my identity. My thinking was that if I could prove it to everyone else, I would definitely finally prove it to myself.

Of course, this was just another version of what I had been doing before. It had everything to do with pushing myself to my absolute limit and reaching for unattainable perfection. Somehow I thought that by being chained to this pursuit of competing in a fitness competition, I would finally break free of my eating disorder. I assumed that by being hypercontrolled, as well as monitored by a coach to ensure I didn't mess up, I would finally be able to eat like a "normal" person and not be cycling through dieting and bingeing nonstop. But I was wrong. Boy, was I wrong.

On the day of the event I stood at the edge of the stage peering past the large burgundy curtains; the velvet felt soft in my hands. I squinted away from the bright lights overhead and cameras flashing from the audience. I could hear the roar of the crowd as women in tiny rhinestone-bedazzled bikinis posed for the panel of judges. Their skin was painted in orange spray tan. I noticed the gigantic fake boobs, with the bikini tops covering just the nipples.

What the fuck am I doing? I asked myself. I had worked my ass off for eight months in order to be thinner and more muscular than I had ever before because this was how I intended to prove my worth to myself. But as I looked in the mirror backstage at my sparkly bikini and spray-on tan, I didn't recognize myself.

This time had slowly broken me down, distancing me from my heart and increasing my hatred of my body. I can remember counting out six almonds—no more and no less—and savoring each one. A few times I ate eight whole almonds, and immediately berated myself for having no willpower. *You're going to ruin your chances of winning*, I told myself.

The truth was, on the day of the competition, I didn't give a fuck about winning. All I wanted to do was get off the stage and put this behind me. I wanted to completely erase the last eight months of my life.

The whole journey was driven by fear. Every single thing I did, day in and day out for those eight months, was driven by this ruthless obsession with my body. I believed that I needed to be perfect to be loved. I needed to be validated to feel like I was worthy. The goals that I manufactured in my mind were driving me into deeper states of pressure and self-hatred, and into disconnection from myself and from my body. I was searching everywhere but inside of me for fulfillment.

I had spent all this time restricting my diet, working out for two hours per day, and saying no to nearly every invite to spend time with friends, and there I stood, with more self-pity and disgust than I'd ever had. I observed my sunken eyes, my ribs protruding from my sides, and my boobs small and saggy.

"Number five, you're up!" the woman backstage yelled.

I glanced down at the plastic button on my bikini and made my way over. I am no stranger to the stage, but before this moment I had been judged on my talent during my childhood and teen years as a dancer. As I walked on the stage I was flooded with shame, as I was acutely aware that this time I was being judged solely on the lack of cellulite in my ass.

The stage lights were blinding. I squinted as I plastered a fake smile on my face. The music blasted as I rotated in the poses. My dad was in the audience, and I thought about how this experience, me standing on this stage, would soon be added to his list of regular joke material, things I would hear for the rest of my life. My dad attended every single dance competition I'd ever done, and joking around was our thing, but he had always been so proud of my athletic ability and talent. But I wasn't proud of myself that day.

The four women on stage held hands and bowed to the audience as they cheered. I could hear screams of my name in between the claps and hollers. So, I won the fitness competition. No win had ever been less satisfying. One by one each sparkly bikini-clad contestant left the stage.

As soon as I was out of view of the audience and judges, I ripped off my stripper heels and ran to the changing room. I opened my bag and tore into packages of dark chocolate almonds and licorice and binged like never before.

It had been so long since I'd had even a gram of sugar, and I was in a trance, tossing handful after handful in my mouth until both bags were completely empty. I sat on the floor of the changing room as women were coming in and out. I peeled off my fake lashes, put my sweatpants on over my bikini, and began to cry. Tears ruined my orange spray tan. They were relentless, as if every emotion I had suppressed was now being released. I didn't hold back. I let myself break down, and as quickly as I felt pain, I buried it with food.

For eight months I had white-knuckled my way through controlling my life by controlling my body. I only had one goal: to get to my ideal weight, and nothing would stand in my way. I ignored everything else in my life. Everything I did was in pursuit of this one incredibly destructive goal that took over my entire life, stripped me of my joy, and spun me deeper into my obsession with food. I was going to be the very best. I was going to win, and in order to do that I was going to deny myself any kind of feeling until I got there. I was not just going to be good enough, I was going to be perfect.

I entered this competition so that I could get better from my eating disorder, so that I could become healthy. And something inside me told me the only way to get healthy was to be perfect at it.

Perfectionism is a bitch. It's debilitating—that feeling of wanting to make a move but being completely paralyzed. Afraid to be wrong, afraid to fail, afraid of not being loved unless everything is completely under our control. Anything less is failure.

This is so very common. I work with clients all the time who encounter this exact same problem. Since when did we decide that the things we did had a direct impact on our worthiness, on our innate self-worth? We halt, we procrastinate, we fail to launch—all because we are deeply afraid of not being good enough.

Perfectionism is the voice we hear on the regular. It's the relentless whisper that drives us into a state of extreme hustle. We hustle for our worth in hopes that someday we will reach the ultimate shining goal of "perfect"—showered in love and honored with respect.

It doesn't work, of course. Our extreme state of hustle never lands us where we actually want to be. The image in our mind of all that love and respect doesn't occur because it isn't a realistic expectation. Perfect is never attainable, and so we always land at not good enough. And if we are not good enough, then no amount of attention or accolades can make up for it. And so we either hustle more, thinking the next goal will be the one, or we collapse in our failure to become perfect. It is a vicious cycle.

All dieters know this feeling. You plunge yourself wholesale into a diet and it goes well for a short period of time until you eat some candy in a thoughtless moment or eat a roll at a restaurant. And then it's like you've flipped a switch: You throw in the towel and eat down the house because you've already failed at being perfect. You are essentially saying to yourself: *I'm either going to be perfect at this, or I am not going to do it at all.*

Now stay with me here. You may be sitting there thinking, *I am not a perfectionist; look at all the ways I am failing in my life right now.* But that would be your perfectionism talking. Because here's the thing about perfectionism: The struggle to be perfect is so insistent that any tiny mistake seems like complete and utter failure. So you are in a constant loop of working too hard and then shutting everything down.

This all-or-nothing mentality is a classic trap. When we buy into the idea that we have to be perfect, and then shut down when inevitably something goes wrong, we completely fail to see all the good we have accomplished.

Take a moment to reflect on the last time you reached one of your body weight goals. Think about a time when you clawed and struggled your way through a diet and finally achieved your goal weight. How did it feel? Were you flying with an abundance of love and light? Did you finally feel loved and worthy at the deepest level? I can guarantee the answer is no. You likely felt a rush of triumph looking down at the scale or the measuring tape. And yes, a momentary rush is wonderful—but, ultimately, you feel depleted. Maybe you have mastered the achievement, but you missed the boat on the fulfillment.

In my experience, that goal weight lasts about five minutes, until you take a deep breath and the weight comes back. Perfect is a fleeting, unsustainable state of being. Ultimately, trying to obtain the perfect body is always a futile task. Each time your weight goes up by a single pound, you sink deeper and deeper into a state of feeling like a complete failure.

Of course, weight naturally fluctuates based on a whole host of factors. It's not possible to stay at that perfect goal weight. But we demand this perfection nevertheless, and so we believe we are worthless when we can't achieve it.

I was convinced I was a failure. My perfectionism told me so—a voice inside. My perfectionism told me I had no willpower, that I was weak. The interesting thing was, this belief—this story about myself—wasn't just about dieting. Not only would I never get the body I wanted, but I would never find love or fulfillment in work. It was as if once I decided I was a failure in this one way, my brain tried its best to prove to me the other ways this was also true. This story bubbles over into every area of our lives. It tears through our self-confidence, driving it into the ground.

Perfectionism is exhausting. It's an unending quest to be anything other than what we are—the perfect mother, the perfect partner, the perfect daughter, the perfect employee, the perfect friend—perfect in every aspect of our lives. Perfectionism makes us feel the weight of the world on our shoulders, not just around our middles and our thighs. Perfectionism forces us to wear masks that fundamentally aren't designed for us, yet we adapt these masks to show the world a false, idealized version of who we are instead of our true selves.

Not only is the journey of achieving exhausting, but the destination itself is often limited and deflating. Let's look at the journey of dieting: Most diets start from a place of hatred. We hate our bodies and we want to change them. Many dieters have decided that their body isn't acceptable—it's too fat or too weak—and there is no way they can possibly be happy living in that body without changing it. We decide we want to take action to make a drastic change. We are motivated by the fear that we will never be happy. But diets and exercise plans that run on fear tire us out pretty quickly and, for the dieter, the shame just heaps on.

But when we shift our perspective and draw motivation from love, the energy of the journey is completely different. It's time to love yourself so fully and graciously that you feel deeply connected to your body, to the point where you understand what your body needs and you nourish it effectively. When you do that, weight loss becomes a result of the care you show your body and the work you put into it, not the entire point of your actions.

When you work toward weight loss from a place of self-love and deep connection to your incredible, useful body, your focus becomes the vision of what you want to create in and about yourself, not what you want to banish, destroy, or control. Have you ever taken a moment and tapped into how you want to feel in your body? Not how you want to look in the mirror or the number you want to see on the scale—how you feel. How do you want to feel as soon as you wake up and throughout your day? The beautiful thing about our bodies is that the energy within them can shift as soon as we shift our focus.

If we are constantly thinking our bodies are disgusting, that they need to be hidden and punished, we are operating constantly from a place of fear and self-judgment. What if we released the fear and allowed ourselves to be motivated by love on the journey to our ideal health?

I've coached tens of thousands of women through this process of weight loss. It's essentially reverse-engineering the process of how we release the weight that has built up on our bodies. Think about how much easier things are in your life when you feel a genuine excitement about the outcome—of feeling good and free. Think about how much expansion you feel in your body, the lightness and certainty you have when you think about completing tasks you know will be fun and worthwhile. Doesn't it make the process so much easier and more enjoyable? What if releasing weight had the same kind of energy around it? What if you were excited about the process and the journey of releasing the excess weight off your body? How would that change your experience? Instead of fearing the long hours of work, why not look forward to trying fun new adventurous classes and cooking up food that nourishes your soul? How would it feel to love and care for your body instead of punishing it and denying it?

Take a moment with me now to create your intention. Imagine feeling at home in your body. What is your posture like when you are feeling your best? What does your facial expression say? How do you feel? Close your eyes, take a deep breath and allow your body to be fully in this picture. Place yourself in that image now as your body is flooded with happiness, worthiness, pride, and possibility.

This is the power of being motivated by love and expansion rather than fear. The perfectionist in us repeats that old saying in our ears—"no pain, no gain"—insisting that it needs to be hard for it to be effective, but we know that's not true. When we operate from fear, all we know is that we are unhappy and we have to fight, kick, and scream to get out of our reality. What if we decided in advance that things can be easy and still be wildly successful? What if we stopped fighting and started loving?

For any true transformation to occur, we first need to start from a place of acceptance of what is, and then find our motivation in love. This likely goes against all the programming you have received from the dieting industry, but it's time to release our addiction to the idea that accomplishment has to be hard. It's time to allow things to be easy. We aren't designed to struggle.

I was caught in the sick illusion that there was such a thing as a perfect body, and that I needed to have it. I was caught in the even sicker illusion that on the "other side" of that perfect body, I would find the love and acceptance I did not feel for myself. Eight months prior to being on that stage I dreamed of the feelings I would be flooded with when I finally made it, when I finally reaped my rewards.

It was a fantasy I created in my head, not based on anything I knew to be true or had previously experienced.

Have you ever heard of a woman reaching her "goal weight" and also fulfilling all of her heart's desires? I certainly haven't. I have worked with women from all over the world, and I have never met one who, after she achieved her goal weight or size, felt sustainably fulfilled deep down for the long term. This way of thinking is a trap.

This entire idea is perpetuated by the weight-loss industry. It promises you the world, that all your dreams will come true when you buy the shake, bottle of pills, detox tea, or tummy wrap and finally become that ideal of a skinny person lounging on a beach featured in the advertisements. This is the illusion we are all buying into. I don't know about you, but each time I finished a diet and reached the "goal weight," I didn't feel like a model on a beach. I felt depleted, terrified of going backward once I had clawed my way to that point.

It's time to rise up and investigate how these illusions and false promises are keeping us stuck. It's time to rise up and allow love to direct the ship. We love from the inside out—not from the outside in. You will watch your world transform into something so much more potent, so much more powerful, and so much more alive once you accept that you do not need to look a certain way to be lovable, wanted, and perfect—you already are.

✦ ✦ ✦

Comparing yourself to other people is perfectionism's equally soul-crushing sidekick. They go hand in hand, working together to convince you that you will never "get there"—whether you are looking at the bikini-clad model in the ads for weight-loss programs, the social media star of the moment, or people in your own life who just seem to have their shit together. We are driven by perfectionism, ego, and the high standards we set for ourselves and when we see someone doing it better, we raise the bar even higher, setting our standard somewhere in impossible-land. And then when we don't reach those goals, we add a chapter to the never-ending "I am not good enough" story. Another vicious cycle begins again.

I don't think I'm the only girl in the world who has taken an innocent little scroll through Instagram and ended up feeling like a giant pile of shit. These airbrushed and filtered little trips through other people's lives make me feel like I will never be able to land in a place where I feel worthy—*I will never have that wealth, body, partner, etc.* But here is the truth: At the end of the day, we all want to feel seen, heard, and loved, and our constantly refreshing social media feeds make it all the easier to go about it in the wrong way. Our phones and computers make it easy to fall down into a well of comparisons, usually when we have a little downtime on a crappy day. We are constantly comparing our everyday lives—lived in real time with bad days and good mixed together—to someone's carefully chosen and planned highlight reel. Sometimes I take a scroll through my own Instagram and think to myself, *Damn, girl, you're cool.* But the truth is that I have the same external struggles and rotten days as you—and so does everyone else, including those Instagram-perfect people. They're just not showing the bad days.

Once we understand the images and personas the people we follow have created are heavily curated personal brands—not the actual interior messy lives of individuals who surely have complicated relationships with food as well—we can move through and out of these illusions.

And even when we know that on a mental level, it's not always easy to soothe the green beast of envy. Ending the quest for some impossible perfection fueled by comparisons to airbrushed influencers and celebrities is a conscious choice. Remember: The weight-loss industry wants nothing more than for you to fall prey to your own self-criticism and weakness.

The majority of women in our culture hate their bodies, and the weight-loss industry capitalizes on this fact. As long as we hate ourselves, we will continue to look for a "magic" cure. We will throw money at that hope and endure all kinds of hardship to achieve some physical shape that we think we can love, starving and punishing our bodies in the process. We are convinced that we've not tried it all yet, so we continue the search—the next miracle pill, the next cleanse, the next trend that will be the golden ticket to have us dancing around like the happy, skinny women in commercials. The fundamental reason the majority of weight-loss programs don't work long term is simply because they play on people's insecurities and false hopes. That will never be the way to create lasting change.

Once we understand the game this industry is playing, we can refuse to play by its rules and play a new one. That new game means loving yourself so fiercely you transcend all efforts to make you feel like you're not perfect and whole exactly as you are, because you are, just as you are, right in this moment. In the thick of my battle with food and my body, my perfectionism was at an all-time high. I genuinely thought I could "shame myself skinny." I was convinced that the harder I was on myself, the quicker I was going to get to my "ideal" weight. I just needed to force harder, restrict more, be an even more raging bitch to myself. I couldn't let go of the hate, because if I did, I was afraid I would spin out of control and soon I would be the very worst version of myself.

We justify these behaviors by convincing ourselves and the world that perfectionism is the road to success. We are convinced it is healthy to lay the hammer down on ourselves day after day when, in fact, nothing could be less healthy. Often our perfectionist tendencies are easily justified by using the term *health*. I see it all the time. "But it's for health reasons!" I can sniff that excuse out a mile away. I myself have used it time and time again. Every diet I was on, I masked as a "health kick," when really it was another desperate attempt to banish the last five pounds I was determined to strip off of my body. The underlying question at the core of a person taking action for genuine health reasons would be "How can I improve?" while a perfectionist takes action because there is a core fear of "What will they think?" This is the difference between taking action from a place of love and taking action from a place of fear.

Perfectionism is a shield, but at a certain point it stops protecting and becomes a barrier between us and the world. We refuse to admit we are human, and this is our flaw. We refuse to allow ourselves to see that we are flawed and perfect at the same time. According to a perfectionist, it's either one or the other, the two cannot coexist. Perfectionists assume their shield will protect them when, in reality, it's the very thing keeping them from growing and fulfilling their potential.

Perfectionism embodies the notion and deep belief that our worth is outside of who we are at our core, dismissing our innate light and power, as if who we are is dependent on how we look, what we accomplish, and how well we accomplish it. This externalization of self-worth means your self-worth is always on the line. It's a never-ending battle and there will always be a new benchmark. When, invariably, we do experience shame, judgment, and blame—which are just part of life—we believe it's because we aren't perfect enough. So rather than questioning the faulty logic of perfectionism, we become even more entrenched in our quest to live, look, and do everything just right. To achieve that elusive goal of perfection that is always just out of reach.

Perfectionists are hypercritical of ourselves, and so by default we become extremely critical of others. We might not even realize that when we are body-shaming ourselves to death, we also are doing it to others. We compare, measure up, and create unrealistic standards for others, just like we do for ourselves. We are quick to see ourselves as "better" or "worse" than others. This creates a lack of intimacy and connection with those who mean the most to us, because energetically we are distancing ourselves from them. We fear being seen, because we fear they will see the broken parts of us. And so we are careful to keep them at arm's length.

So what if we are messy, cluttered, and make mistakes? What if we gave ourselves permission to fuck up and love ourselves anyway? How much freedom would we have then? What if we knew, deep in our soul really knew, that *doing* all the time doesn't allow us to feel more love? What if we knew instead that simply *being* allows us all the love we could ever need?

What if we stopped hustling and started accepting? What if we could deeply love ourselves in the midst of our perceived imperfections and mess? What if you could love yourself for the beautiful mess you are? Embracing all of you, loving each part with grace, hugging the parts of you that are scared, rather than hustling to ignore them. This is true self-love. This is where real transformation happens.

What if you allowed yourself to bask in self-acceptance? What if you could forgive yourself for every mistake, knowing that it was just a part of your path? What if you made it easy to drench yourself in the love you so desperately deserve?

Nothing stalls greatness like perfectionism. Aim for good enough for today, just for now, and chances are you will land in greatness almost by accident.

"I'll make better mistakes tomorrow," is a mantra I keep on a sticky note on my bathroom mirror. It allows me to explore, experience, and play in life without it feeling so serious, without the pressure of needing to do things a certain way in order to feel successful. Some of my greatest memories and lessons exist within the times when everything felt messy and dissolved. Make mistakes, get messy, and allow all of it to exist in a perfect balance.

INTEGRATIVE PRACTICE

Meditation: Better Mistakes Tomorrow

I want you to repeat the following phrases over and over, saying all six and then starting back at the beginning. You can sit in a comfortable position and set a goal for a number of repetitions, or simply set a timer. There is no way to be perfect at this mantra meditation, so make the timer or the number goal easy and sustainable. Make this practice something that it would be a joy to come back to regularly. Start with a very small goal like one minute or three repetitions, and when you come back to this exercise, try going up by one repetition or one minute.

- I am in the process of learning to love and accept myself just as I am.

- I am in the process of understanding that no one and nothing is perfect.

- I am in the process of allowing myself love and acceptance.

- I am in the process of understanding that it is my imperfections that make me lovable.

- I am in the process of allowing space for mistakes and learning.

- I will make better mistakes tomorrow.

Journaling: You Are Innately Worthy

You are human, my love, and as such you are innately worthy of love and belonging. If you overeat, miss the gym, or if your house is in a state—you are still inherently worthy.

This deep truth is counterintuitive to a lot of the social conditioning we are exposed to. It's important to push yourself to begin to admit and accept who you already are. Remove yourself from societal norms when it comes to what is lovable and appropriate and create your own path to your deepest self-love and acceptance.

Freewrite and be creative with this exercise using some of the sentence starters:

- When I fully love and accept myself no matter what, I feel . . .

- I know happiness is my natural state because . . .

- My new beliefs around how lovable I am . . .

- I am choosing to release the grip of perfectionism because . . .

- This will allow me to . . .

CHAPTER 5

SOOTHING YOUR INNER CHILD

I loved baths as a kid. I would spend hours and hours soaking and drinking iced chai lattes that Mom made while devouring Sophie Kinsella books. Although I had friends at school and playdates, I craved being alone with my own thoughts and energy. The bath was my escape, the place I could go to be alone. I'd stay in the bath until my icy drink had melted, until the water became cold, and my little fingers shriveled.

At 12 years old, however, I began to notice my body. And I hated it. I would tie sweaters around my waist to hide my ass and wear baggy sweatshirts and jeans. I desperately wanted to be invisible. I would take both hands and pinch my belly until I nearly drew blood, grunting with frustration as shame flooded my body. I felt disgusting. I felt obese. I felt like I didn't belong in this body. Everything in me wanted to escape, to eject myself from this body and land in a body that looked lean, free, and light.

It was around this time that my bath-time ritual lost its glow. Starting from age 12, I would admire my friends' legs-for-days while I compared them to my thicker thighs and cankles. Bath time quickly became a time for me to berate my body, a time for me to wish I was anywhere but stuck in this meat suit. I can't remember a time in my teenage years when I felt comfortable in my body. I can't remember a time I truly relaxed and felt peaceful in my skin. There was always this underlying chaos—this deep unsettling—I could feel in my bones.

I did everything in my power to make sure I was the sole keeper of this body-hatred secret. God forbid I ask for support, or air out my dirty laundry for the world to "fix," for even at age 12 I was ruthlessly committed to making sure I wasn't a nuisance to anyone else. The fear of being a nuisance was a consistent theme for the next 15 years of my life, as I constantly put on what I have come to think of as the "everything-is-awesome" mask and made sure everyone else's needs were met, but never my own. This pattern eventually created a deep resentment in me toward myself and the world.

Little did I know during those precious years that the fear and anxiety I found myself trapped in had nothing to do with my sweet little 12-year-old body. Though I was convinced that dropping a few pounds would land me in a mystical land of contentment, a place where my inner critic would be silenced and my heart would expand, that was never the case. The core of my anger, fear, and self-hatred wasn't curable by simply losing weight.

Many years later, I came across the notion of the inner child. I was visiting some friends in California, and when I asked them about this concept, they looked at me like I had shown up to a party about three hours late. They introduced me to Andrew, an energy healer. The whole thing seemed preposterous to me, but Andrew was a warm, funny, down-to-earth guy, who looked shockingly more like a skater kid than an energy healer. He began to show me that I have an inner child, a version of myself who just never quite got all of her needs met growing up and was still very much alive inside me. In fact, when I really listened, I could locate my inner child physically inside my body.

I could feel the resonance in my heart, and my body could viscerally feel the truth in the words Andrew was saying. It felt so real, so I kept leaning in, and the more I did, the more I learned, and the more I learned, the more I healed. The connection I had with my inner child had a direct impact on my relationship with food. The more I allowed myself to love her, the more I healed.

After that first day of meeting my inner child through Andrew, I hugged him good-bye and drove the backroads back to my Airbnb. The sun was setting and Adele was coming through the speakers. I could feel the calmness of the golden hour as I cruised through the meandering roads. Tears were falling on my lap as I visualized my inner child. *How could I have abandoned her?* I thought. The thought of how I had disconnected from my inner child and completely ignored her needs made me feel sick. I pictured myself as a little girl—so joyful, excited, and full of love. Any chance I could, I was singing and dancing and bursting with life. I knew that version of me still existed. I knew she was still there.

Since this experience of meeting my inner child, I have come to the conclusion that there is no such thing as an adult, we are all just tall children. If you're reading this thinking, *Whoa, this is way too out there for me*, I hear you—I felt the same way. But hang on with me here, and I promise this will be life changing.

Do you ever have moments in life when your emotions get the best of you and you freak out? Those moments in life when you are immediately ashamed and think to yourself, *I can't believe I just did that? I can't believe I just said that?* These moments are reactions of your inner child. Your inner child is having a shit fit because she feels ignored, and when this happens, we often take the needs of our unmet selves and project them onto a loved one, a colleague, or even a stranger who does the smallest thing to annoy us.

When you yell at someone, or when you choose to project your problems onto them, remember one very important concept: If you feel like you cannot survive unless someone else meets your need, this is actually a need your inner child is demanding from you. It might often sound like this: *Why are you not listening to me? Why are you always ignoring me? What is wrong with you that you are acting like this?*

That desperate feeling of *someone has to meet my needs right now* is how you know it's coming from your inner child. And when you think about it that way, it helps to understand how you can get stuck in a cycle of binge eating and restricting.

You'll hear me say time and time again that "it's not about the food," but during my own recovery this was a hard concept to understand. *What do you mean it's not about the food? Food is ruining my life, it's all I think about, all I obsess over—I can't even think straight when food is around. Of course it's about the food.*

But it's really, really not.

Chances are your inner child is desperately asking for your attention, begging to be heard and understood, begging to be listened to and loved. Your inner child has needs that you aren't meeting right now, and therefore your body is responding in sensations, usually sensations of anxiety, pain, and overwhelm. When these sensations are active, we reach for food to numb them, to diffuse the pain. This is how food becomes a drug, how food addiction starts. We don't have the tools to understand and heal our emotions, so rather than feel them, we numb them and move on.

For the majority of the women and men I've worked with, the thing they want is comfort. To feel comfortable in their body, comfortable around food, and comfortable with their emotions. Binge eating is a strategy to feel that comfort, though of course it is destructive. I call these "shitty strategies." This type of strategy is a way to get your needs met in a dopamine-hitting, instant-satisfaction kind of way, but it's not sustainable and just leaves you feeling worse on the other side.

What are you truly hungry for? What does your inner child need? Does she need love, comfort, adventure, peace, slowness, nourishment? Creating healthy strategies to meet these needs is an act of love. Taking the time to understand what you need on a visceral level, and being intentional about meeting those needs on a daily basis, will be one of the greatest shifts you can possibly make.

When I tell my clients that the relationship they have with food is a blessing, they look at me as if I've just dropped acid, but it's the truth. Binge eating and emotional eating are not about the food, not even a little. Remember: Pain and emotions are data, they are your body's way of telling your mind what you need. It's just that sometimes your body and your mind are not used to communicating with one another, so there can be a bit of a learning curve when you are first working to connect the two.

Emotions drive behavior. We have a feeling in our body, which causes the mind to create a reason for the feeling and then a solution. I'm going to take a wild guess and suggest that the clever solution your mind decides on when encountering an emotion that makes it uncomfortable is hinting that you should have a snack, because that always makes you feel better. In other words, your solution to discomfort is emotional eating. On your way home from an awkward first date, it can feel like second nature to grab a pint of ice cream to eat on the couch or to treat yourself to a bag of cookies after a rough day at work. That was certainly my go-to solution on the regular.

The root problem isn't the emotional eating. The problem is the ignored emotion. Instead of eating, have you asked yourself: How did the date go wrong and how do you feel about it? What was bothering you at work and what can you change? When we see emotions as a messenger and listen closely to their message, they can be a beautiful tool to let us know what our inner child needs. This requires convincing the mind to listen, feel, and sit with the information given to us by our emotions—no matter how challenging the feelings that bubble up or the dark places we might find ourselves. Emotional pain is the indicator light that there is something going on that we are ignoring. Very often this kind of pain is a whisper from our inner child, a whisper about needs that are not being met.

I assumed the path of coming home to my inner child and meeting her needs would be tumultuous and treacherous. I assumed it would be a challenge that would take me years to master and, being the perfectionist I was, I thought I needed to soothe and heal my inner child perfectly, or not at all. Looking back, it's clear that I avoided dealing with these issues not just because I didn't want to face the pain, but because I knew I didn't yet have the tools and the time to dedicate to healing fully. But I soon discovered that the path to healing my inner child was simple. That isn't to suggest it was easy. It is not easy to honor a difficult process, and certainly not easy to honor the needs of an inner child who needs a whole lot of love, but what is simpler than love, really? Like I said: simple, but not easy.

As a child, my nickname was Sammy Whammy after my wild antics that often had me literally bouncing off the walls. And during my journey of coming back home to her, it's how I referred to my inner child. It's funny, I know, but here is why I do it: I use this nickname to remind me of how cute my five-year-old self was, tearing around the house light and joyous. So innocent and trusting of the world. When I think of her that way, it's really hard to be mean to her. It is really hard to see myself as someone I need to shame into being skinny when I am calling her Sammy Whammy.

Sometimes when I feel my inner child acting out and insisting on some shitty strategy that I know won't work for me, I picture Sammy Whammy throwing a temper tantrum. She was set off by something she saw as unfair. I picture this little girl who was me and somewhere inside still is me, and I think, *How can I help that little girl feel better?* This process was a lot slower than I initially assumed— because it's hard to know sometimes what sets off a kid— but it was a lot simpler, too. I asked her multiple times a day, "How can I love you more?" and "What do you most need right now?"

I was shocked by how the answers that rose up inside me were so obvious and came so quickly. It was often something like, "Please slow down, please give me rest." Or she would say, "Let me play." "Let me say what I want to say." Or sometimes, "I don't want to be friends with that person anymore—it hurts me to be around her." Or, "Call Amy.

I want to feel connected to my best friend." Sometimes I was shocked to hear something very vulnerable and simple, like, "Tell me you love me and you're listening to me."

It's beautiful to take the time to ask these questions. It's a true act of love for ourselves. Self-love is often talked about, but rarely practiced. This is a beautiful start to this practice and, if you allow it, it will fulfill you in ways you never knew possible. Allow the love to flow through your body and heal what needs to be healed. Love truly is a healing energy. It allows the painful parts of our body to soften, it allows our mind to find elements of peace, and it allows our heart to feel our true essence.

Take a moment with me right now. I want to show you the power of this practice, the power of coming home to yourself and being with your inner child. Take a deep breath, and another, and another. Close your eyes, visualize your inner child, and say, "I love you, I'm listening," over and over again. If only I had access to these practices as a 12-year-old in the bathtub, I could have saved myself over a decade of suffering.

Here is the thing: You don't need to obsess over letting go of the shitty strategies, the old ways you used to meet your needs. You just need to focus on creating new strategies. Once you have better, more empowering strategies in place, the old ones that aren't serving you will simply release.

It gets to be simple. Who said transformation always needs to be painful and difficult? Yes, sometimes moving through some emotional blocks can feel scary and challenging, but we can choose to see this as an adventure. We can choose to be empowered by that which challenges us.

Understanding who we are and what really lights us up from within is a beautiful task. Here's the interesting thing: The majority of humanity has no idea what lights them up. They have no idea what they want. But when we move into a place of being intentional about creating our experience, we have the space and awareness to create the life we want based on what we actually desire. Halle-freaking-lujah.

I used to think a binge or even just five uncomfortable or painful minutes would mean my entire day was ruined. I would throw in the towel that the other 23 hours and 55 minutes of the day were worthless. I was convinced I couldn't turn the train around. What I now know to be true is that we have the ability to change our focus, and ultimately our state of mind and emotions, in an instant. We just need to know how powerful our ability to choose really is.

The most powerful lesson I learned as I explored my relationship with Sammy Whammy was that I could choose how I felt. Somehow it had never occurred to me before, but during this process I learned to hold two conflicting emotions inside of me at once. I had developed the habit of choosing to suffer over healing—choosing the hard path, the familiar path, the painful path. You can feel love and pain, joy and shame, anxiety and bliss. It all exists within you. And it is your choice which emotion you experience, which path you walk.

We are often habituated to be all-or-nothing thinkers. Especially us dieters. We are either *so on* the diet, or *so off* the diet. There is no in between. Refusing that simplistic black and white worldview when it comes to your self-understanding opens you up to different opportunities and ways of being. Living in the gray—allowing more than one option of how to exist within ourselves—can truly set us free. This is especially true when it comes to the sensations we feel in our bodies. We are creative beings, we get to create the sensation we desire—we have the power to choose.

Love naturally feels light and expansive within the body. Experiencing self-love feels refreshing and exciting, and the power to choose it is an incredible gift. The more we give our bodies a sip of the good stuff—self-acceptance, nourishment, and love—the more joy and bliss we will experience. Eventually our bodies become acclimatized to these feelings, allowing the sensation of self-acceptance to be the rule instead of the exception.

When we allow ourselves to exist in a state of joy, we have deeper access to our inner child. She opens up and she allows us in. You are coming home to the most important relationship in your adult life. You are becoming the nurturer that you have always needed. Your attention is the medicine your inner child craves, and your love is the nourishment to meet her needs. Allow this process to be gentle and sweet. Be the parent for that part of you that still needs one—we all have that need, no matter how old we are.

INTEGRATIVE PRACTICE

Coming home to your inner child is a beautiful process, but it takes a lot of kindness, patience, and understanding. If you abandoned your inner child long ago, it's going to take a while for the two of you to reconnect. Don't rush this process or expect the connection to happen quickly. Be gentle, be open, and allow the body to decide the time line for establishing connection, not the mind. I've had thousands of clients give up because this connection hasn't come quickly enough. Don't fall into this trap. Remember, the body has a different time line than the mind does, and the body will process and heal in the way that is most nurturing. Trust it. Your job is to show up for your inner child and practice extreme self-compassion and kindness.

Meditation: Honoring the Inner Child

When you wake up in the morning, take a few minutes for this exercise. First, connect and say good morning to your inner child. Perhaps you have a nickname or a special candle that you light when you want to reach for your inner child. Ask your inner child what she is longing for today.

Now feel for the sensation your inner child wants you to step into that day. Then remember and imagine what it is like to hold that emotion in your body. Think of images that remind you of being free or happy or playful or whatever it is your inner child wants you to feel that day. Let the sensation flood your body. Then, throughout the day, when you find yourself in another emotion, reach for the bodily sensations of the emotion your inner child suggested for that day and choose it instead. You may face challenges, but the commitment you make to yourself in your morning meditation is that you can continue to choose.

Journaling: Write a Letter to Your Inner Child

Before you begin this exercise, take a moment to ask your body what it needs in this moment. Say the words, "How can I love you more? How can I help you to get what you are really craving?" Notice how your body shifts into presence when this happens. What are you truly hungry for? What does your inner child need? Does she need love, comfort, peace, slowness, nourishment? Adventure, excitement, playfulness, a chance to be creative, a chance to feel free, a chance to feel empowered?

In this exercise we are going to be writing a letter to your inner child, a letter that lets your inner child know how sorry you are for abandoning her, for neglecting her needs and not truly loving her. Your letter is a letter of reclamation, a letter to let her know she is free to be heard, seen, and loved. Here are a few things to include:

- Let her know how sorry you are for abandoning her. Apologize.

- Let her know you're learning. Ask for forgiveness.

- Let her know she is now safe to have a voice and be heard. Commit to listening and being the parent she has always craved.

- Let her know it's safe to express, play, and experience the joy in life.

- Let her know how excited you are to reconnect with her.

These are just a few jumping-off points to get you started. Allow this process to be creative and conducive to what feels best for you. Take your time, light a candle, put on some music, and do a simple body scan meditation before beginning to write your letter, so you are beautifully grounded and the words can flow out of you effortlessly. Write directly from the heart.

CHAPTER 6

EMOTIONAL MASTERY

Most people have high standards for their external lives and low standards for their internal lives. We are busy buying expensive cars, dreaming of beachfront homes, and booking vacations on credit cards so it looks like we have our shit together, all while we are denying the very core of what creates happiness, denying our mental and emotional well-being. We spend ungodly amounts of time proving ourselves to others, showing that we are important and that we matter, but we are missing the point completely. Not only do we deny our inner worlds—we straight up suppress them, numbing their signals and messages out with food and other distractions. And then we wake up and wonder why we feel like shit.

Humor me for a moment: What if you spent more time paying attention to raising your internal standards rather than hustling to make sure your external world looked acceptable to your followers on social media? What would shift within you? What would shift in your external world?

Being a human can really be a mindfuck if we don't understand how we are fundamentally designed. We are dealing with two different operating systems simultaneously. First, we have our two-million-year-old survival brain, that part of our internal dialogue screaming at us to "watch out," keeping us in a constant state of overwhelm and fear. But the second part of our internal dialogue, our intuition, is that clear voice of reason. It's our true north, the part of us that always knows our next move and is always guiding us on our path. The problem here is the fact that the intuition is impossible to access when we are riddled with fear. It gets drowned out by the screams of the survival brain.

In order to tap into the divine guideline of our intuition, we need to observe our thoughts without validating them and letting them take over the narrative, so we can be set free from the noise and chaos in the mind. Then and only then will we tap into the clear guidance of our intuition. Essentially, the happiness hack here is understanding how to have a relationship with our thoughts so we don't fight them, and they don't fight us. When we simply observe and inquire, we can have space from the chatter, noise, and drama that is trapped between our ears.

Most people don't realize how much power they truly have over their emotional state. After coaching thousands of women and men, I've seen the same patterns over and over again. Humans are fairly predictable. People allow external circumstances to dictate the internal. Instead of making a conscious decision about how they want to feel and shifting their internal state in that direction, they allow external circumstances—like stress at work or trouble in a relationship—to drive the bus without even realizing that the keys were in their hands the whole time.

Wayne Dyer said, "When you change the way you look at things, the things you look at change." We live in a world where we are so busy trying to control and change the external forces in our lives so that we feel better, we end up in an endless loop, never feeling like we've "made it." When is enough ever going to be enough? In this journey of keeping up with the Joneses and aiming for perfection, who is going to wave the flag and congratulate us that thanks to all of our hustle and self-hatred, we've landed in the destination we call "happiness"? No one. Because life doesn't work like that.

Take a minute and get clear on the emotions you want to feel every day, whether that is contentment, safety, acceptance, love, or strength. Breathe and feel this now. You know how to create this feeling. It's simple: Take a moment of calm and clarity to go to a place inside where you store the memory of a comforting embrace, the moment you found out some amazing news, or just a beautiful, simple moment that crystallized in your mind and your senses. Your ability to focus inward is an incredibly powerful tool. Use those powerful thoughts of yours to fill yourself with the desired feeling. If love is your desired feeling, it's important to have clear imagery of what creates that feeling within your body. Focus on a specific situation in the past, or on something you're intent on creating in the future. Choose a moment, scene, or image that fills you with so much love that you are at the point where your heart feels cracked wide open, deeply loving. Was it that first moment you saw your child? The moment you said "I do" to your spouse? Or is it a scene in your favorite novel or film that you will never forget?

When we are highly intentional with our focus in this way, we begin to shift into that vibration. This is called a focus field. We are creating a field of energy surrounding the vibrations we choose to operate within. And the beautiful thing about this is, the more we are in this state of focus, the more we attract situations into our life that match this vibration. Like attracts like, and it's the same with energy—we attract what we are. Happiness attracts happiness and pain, pain. We attract what we feel.

Make the image within your focus field brighter, breathing and feeling deeper. Can you feel your body literally shifting as you read these words? Can you feel your frequency increasing? Keep going. Allow yourself to be completely surrounded by that heart-cracked-wide-open feeling just by using your thoughts. Allow yourself to savor this moment, relish in it—allow it to consume your entire experience. Feels juicy, light, and beautiful, doesn't it? And you know what is amazing? Nothing in the external world changed. You didn't need to fight for this feeling, you didn't need to "prove" yourself, hustle, or try to be something or someone that you aren't. You just gave yourself permission to feel. You chose to change yourself from the inside out.

You just created a feedback loop of high vibrational energy. The more you create the thoughts in your mind, the more your body is flooded with high vibrational energy, and the more your body is vibrating at that level, the more beautiful, inspiring thoughts you'll have.

But here is the kicker, my friend: It works in the opposite way as well. Just as you created high vibrational energy with positive thoughts, you can create the opposite dynamic of low vibrational energy with negative thoughts. And in fact, you're probably doing it all the time, as are the people around you. We all unconsciously give off energy all day long. Each of us is constantly flooded with sensations from the world around us—absorbing the worries, fears, and potential catastrophes of others. When we don't take control of these thoughts, we can internalize them and become overwhelmed with fears borrowed from other people. We then operate in a fearful state, not based on what is true for us, but based on what people are thinking and feeling around us.

I want you to take a moment to be with the hatred you have for your body and the fears you have around food. As we move through this exercise, I want you to know you're safe. It is completely safe in this moment to feel emotions that you may be pushing down. We need to feel our emotions, so we don't feed them.

This is one of those times that the old adage "the only way out is through" rings particularly true. The only way out of the battle with food and your body is to come to terms with the emotions that you have been pushing down for so long. You can't continue to numb these emotions by bingeing or by restricting your body into submission. The intention here is to observe the feelings, the thoughts, and the impulses without judgment or trying to shut them down immediately. Think the thoughts, feel the emotions. Don't worry, you are just the observer of these sensations. They will not consume you, for you are much more powerful and influential than your thoughts. Feel the fear all the way through without trying to change it.

Now I want you to notice the part of yourself that is observing these emotions. Notice the part of you that is scared of these feelings. Maybe you have made up a story that if you feel them, you'll get stuck forever and never get out, sinking into the pain and confusion like quicksand. I get it—I've been there. I also drummed up that kind of nonsense in my mind. But remember, it's just energy, just emotion; it's not you. You are safe to observe and to feel the full spectrum of your feelings because you are in control. In fact, the more we feel into these emotions, the more we can heal them. That's the core principle of this work. Feel as deeply as you can, open up to the sensation. I know this might feel intense and perhaps even scary, but as we have been discovering, pain is the portal to the truth.

I now want you to imagine yourself in a body that feels light and peaceful—a representation of your true self. Allow yourself to create a version of you without any lack or limitation. Allow yourself to truly explore the body you see for yourself, but most important, the desired feeling that accompanies that body. Breathe into that feeling and allow it to consume your body completely. Once you're there, take it a step further and increase the feeling by being grateful for its presence in your body. Gratitude is the amplifier of all greatness, and by transforming your goal body and mind-set into a source of that gratitude and potential instead of pain and self-hatred, you will reach that greatness. It's incredible the level of control we have to create a positive, inspirational internal landscape and how quickly we can tap into this state with natural ease.

I felt the fire gently warming my feet as I cuddled into the chesterfield with my cup of herbal tea and flannel blanket. This was one of those moments in life when things just felt perfect—a moment I stored away for myself to focus on when I need to feel gratitude, acceptance, and love. I took a deep breath as I watched the flames dance across the logs, my heart expanding with each burst of laughter and chattering women's voices from the retreat attendees seated around me.

Being immersed in a small group of women lights up my soul in ways the person I used to be—the person who would surround herself with bags of chips and candy like a protective barrier—didn't even know were possible. She never imagined that she could ever be on the other side of her food issues and at peace, let alone leading other women as they healed.

But mixed with the joy in my body, I also felt sadness. I thought about each one of the women I was working with, and felt for the child that still existed within each of them. I could feel the endless love that poured out of them in the way they listened and supported one another, in their laughter and their caring exchanges. I could see it so clearly, it made me wonder: *Why don't they see the power of their own love? Why are they so hard on themselves? Why do they hate their bodies? They offer each other so much love, how can they offer themselves this same kind of acceptance? Why can't they feel the love I feel for them, for themselves?*

As we came back into session, we gathered around the fire and I looked at each of them in silence. I looked into the eyes of these women and saw pure love. I asked, "On a day-to-day basis, what are you most focused on?"

The answers were painful to hear, but not surprising given the deep work we were there to do. "How much I hate my body." "The guilt from everything I've been over-eating." "The fact that I am a horrible mother." "How I can never keep up with anything." "How I am so far behind in life, I feel like a failure."

"What if you focused on your heart?" I said. "What if you focused on how magnificent you are, how you have a beautiful body that guides this experience? What if you were to take the time to focus on where you wanted to go, and how capable you are of achieving it? What if you were to focus on your desires, knowing with all your heart that you are so deserving of all the love you deeply crave?"

They all stared back at me, looks of inspiration and confusion in equal parts.

Humans are simple creatures, we really are. But we do a really good job at complicating life and making happiness this challenge we all must strive for. It's bullshit. There were 16 women in the circle, and each had a primary focus on her fears or negative self-belief, a focus which led to an internal state of distress, anxiety, and pain. They epitomized the vibrational feedback loop tuned to the negative frequency, radiating that pain out into every area of their lives and their worlds. When our driving focus is negative and punishing, voiced by our inner critic, we are tapped into a lower frequency. When we allow our bodies to operate on that low frequency on a regular basis, it becomes normal and accepted. And even if it's complete garbage, those hateful "I am a failure" thoughts start to feel like the truth when they are thought over and over again.

Changing that focus takes intention. It takes presence and it takes choosing.

Throughout my years as a coach, CEO, and human being, I've realized that the most successful people in the world—the ones who have mastered the art of fulfillment and being happy—are experts at two things: 1. being happy for no reason; and 2. managing their emotional state. There is a beauty in settling into happiness not because something has shifted in our external world, but simply because we are alive. Being grateful simply because we exist, not because we've won the lottery or hit that perfect dress size or number on the scale. These exceptional people can change their state, choose differently, and know that within each moment they have the ability to focus on what will bring them into an increased energy and a higher frequency, simply by using their thoughts and creating focus fields.

I'm a ninja when it comes to hacking my way to happiness. I'm always asking, "How can I feel freaking incredible without working so hard?" This may seem like laziness, but it isn't. I know that at our cores we are designed for happiness. Love and light are our natural states. So why work so hard? Why put in sweat and effort only to achieve the very thing we are?

When we try to muscle our way to happiness by constantly striving and beating ourselves up at every setback, we are denying the brilliance and magnificence of what we are. It's a slap in the face to the universe that made us perfect, whole, and complete. It's time to raise your standards, release your addiction to the struggle, and choose differently. It's time to rise up and allow yourself to feel the deepest states of fulfillment.

That is how you hack your way to happiness.

It requires stepping out of the addiction to suffering and truly choosing ourselves, choosing to acknowledge our brilliance and let go of the story that we aren't deserving of the highest states of happiness available. It's about understanding our worth and aligning our energy according to that deep knowing. It's about surrendering to ease and giving up the fight.

See, we really are simple creatures. We just need to reset these archaic brains back to their default setting of happiness as opposed to survival, because if we don't, we will be living in a constant state of fear. We need to raise our standards and choose to exist in a frequency that is optimized for happiness.

Decide in advance how you want to feel. Decide in advance to generate positive vibrational energy. And decide the narrative that supports that feeling. When you want to experience the deepest level of abundance, choose a memory from your life that supports that desired feeling—like a holiday table heaped with a feast and surrounded by loved ones, or the moment when you received the first paycheck from a big job—and feel it deeply. Feel grateful for it. It's important to have these decisions made in advance, so that when you feel yourself slipping into a vibration that doesn't support you, you can shift your focus, create a different field, and ultimately change the trajectory of your day. This, done over and over again with enough repetition, will change your entire life.

INTEGRATIVE PRACTICE

Our entire life is driven by how we feel. Everything we do is a reflection of the emotional state we are in when we do it. Energy is truly everything. Being a master at shifting energy is one of the greatest skills we can embody as humans. Being able to feel through the pain and then allowing ourselves to learn from it and move on so it doesn't shift into suffering is a practice that will benefit you greatly.

Journaling: Identifying Emotional Anchors

Emotional anchors are visuals that create emotions within the body, imagery to create the desired focus field. They will help you shift out of the pain so that you don't fall into suffering, toward the happiness you choose to feel instead. In this exercise we will be getting clear on the three emotional sensations we want to experience, as well as the imagery that allows us to experience more of that sensation, freely and effortlessly.

List three feelings you want to feel in your body on a regular basis. It could be happiness, peace, contentment, ease, joy, playfulness, optimism, fulfillment—see what resonates for you.

For each of those three feelings, write down three emotional anchors—or images—that represent that feeling, exploring the emotions that they call up for you. These images can be connected to moments in your past when you felt these emotions, or to imagined moments in your future. They can even be scenes from movies or books—whatever sparks that feeling most deeply, that is the image you should use. These are the images you can turn to when you're feeling pain you no longer need to feel. Use them to change your inner experience.

Meditation: Fixing Emotional Anchors

For each of the three desired feelings you wrote about in your journal, I want you to sit in meditation and create a focus field around you. Set a timer for five minutes. Working with one feeling at a time, bring forth each of the three emotional anchor images you selected for that feeling. Take your time, and immerse yourself fully, allowing yourself to soften into the experience of each anchor before moving on to the next. After the five minutes, start your timer over again and turn your attention to your next desired feeling. Repeat the process of moving through each connected image, fully embodying the feeling that these images spark in you. When these five minutes are up, restart your timer and do it once more, really sealing the deal. You are fixing these emotional anchor images into your brain so that you can draw on them whenever you need them.

CHAPTER 7

THE ANTIDOTE
TO SELF-SABOTAGE

It had been five days of no bingeing. A record during my diet depression era. And I felt like a ticking time bomb. I was holding on for dear life, white-knuckling my way through my days in fear that at any moment I would crack, any moment I would lose control, eat my feelings until I was sick, and then begin the cycle of restricting once again. I sat on my hands and avoided social situations so I could last one more day without using food as a drug. My goal was to make it to seven days, and I didn't want to fuck it all up now. I did whatever I could to avoid situations that might be tempting or cause me to slip into the misery of binge eating.

So I stayed small. I contracted my life around me to make it manageable, or at least that is what I told myself. Words are such effective weapons, and my inner critic was well armed. To drown out the chatter of my own inner dialogue, I busied myself by taking walks multiple times a day, but my mental soundtrack was relentless. All I could hear was: *You're about to cave. What makes you think you'll make it this time? You are too weak to succeed at this. You're about to break at any moment.* I was trying to fight, struggle, and claw myself to normalcy and happiness, even though my inner dialogue wasn't in alignment with my goals. Desperately trying to hustle my way out of my disorder in the only way I knew how was taking all of my concentration.

Unfortunately, that way was flawed. It left me feeling exhausted, like I was always failing—fighting with myself. Sure enough, on the fifth evening I gave in and soothed myself with half a pint of Ben & Jerry's Half Baked ice cream and the embarrassing, painful, and all-too-familiar cycle of addiction started yet again. I sabotaged my own efforts when I had barely begun to make progress.

Self-sabotage isn't what it seems. It isn't about weakness. It's much deeper. It happens when our core beliefs aren't in alignment with our reality. I had clung fiercely to my firmly held belief in my secret identity, claiming, "I am an emotional eater." When I didn't emotionally eat for those five days, it created a discrepancy between my belief and my reality. And the stress and tension that accompanied that discrepancy served as the trigger for my self-sabotage.

When self-sabotage happens, it's usually because a part of us has already decided that we don't have the strength to complete our set goal—we have given up on some level. I can still hear the screams echoing in my head from my diet depression days: *I know everything I need to do, why can't I just do it?* I knew I was smart and that I had the tools and ability to free myself from this cycle. I knew I had mastered the "plan" of how to do it, but I could never stick to that plan.

Little did I know then, but there is an explanation why: The body needs consistency between beliefs and behavior. There needs to be alignment between the two, and if there isn't, we shift our behaviors until we reach a balance. You are not failing at losing weight or changing your habits because you are inherently a failure. You are failing because you *believe* yourself to be a failure.

Think about this: When people win the lottery, what is the story we hear time and time again? That they spent every last dollar within a few years and are now broke again. Is this a coincidence? Not even a little bit. When someone's story around money is: *I am broke, money is hard to make, and hard to keep*, and then millions of dollars land in their lap, those beliefs about money come up against this new rich reality. With most people, their existing belief system wins out. This is exactly what is happening when you attempt to change your behaviors but ignore your beliefs. You end up setting yourself up for failure, sabotaging your efforts before you have even begun.

◆ ◆ ◆

When we start out on a weight-loss plan, some of the most common beliefs at this point are usually: *I am overweight, I have no willpower, I have never successfully done this, I am not worthy enough, I am the "fat girl," I have always been this way, etc*. We almost always start most diets with negative motivations—hating our fat and our bodies and wanting change fueling the fires. Then, from that place of negativity, we try and make a positive change—a change in habits and weight and behavior completely at odds with the beliefs we are holding on to.

The results are usually a hot mess. We find ourselves going back to our old patterns within a few days. There are millions of people operating in this way right in this very second, in a broken model of behavior that leaves them feeling like they don't have the inner power to make a change in their lives. Each time we fail, we prove our beliefs right, confirming the negative assumptions that failure was inevitable, and further widening the gap between belief and reality. This is a sick and twisted illusion, and it's one that I am committed to smashing.

First, we need to address the beliefs driving us. We're not going to focus on behavioral change, but instead on shifting the beliefs that motivate them so that changing behaviors is simply a by-product. In other words: If you believe you can make positive change, then the choices you make will follow.

Everything we do in life is driven by our beliefs. Therefore, if we want to see sustainable, long-term change, we need to first do the inner work and begin our shift from within. When I first learned this during my recovery, I thought it was a load of shit. I wanted change to be quick, forceful, and immediate. Shifting my beliefs sounded like it was going to take forever. I thought all I needed was the right plan and I could summon the will to push through. But when I found myself back on my ass surrounded by the remnants of yet another binge, or crying myself to sleep week after week, I knew I needed a change. I decided to see what this inner-work stuff was all about. Since then I haven't looked back.

That the realities of our lives are a direct reflection of our beliefs is sometimes a hard pill to swallow. I can remember one of my coaches telling me that my bank account was a direct reflection of how much I valued myself and I nearly puked in my mouth. "What is the reality of what you desire in your bank account?" he asked with his piercing blue eyes and monotone voice.

I looked at him and said, "Five hundred thousand dollars." I could feel my stomach clench as I stated these words out loud.

"What do you need to believe about yourself and your value for this to become a reality?"

I searched for the answers, and before my mind was able to consciously connect the dots I blurted out, "That I attract unlimited abundance in each and every moment."

When we deeply believe something to be true, that belief creates thought patterns that "speak" to us. You know the voice in your head? The one that sometimes feels relentless and overbearing? That voice is a function of your most deeply rooted beliefs, nudging you toward alignment with those beliefs in all areas of your life. We can't always see our beliefs for what they are. They may seem invisible and incredibly complex at first, but simply observe your thoughts and you'll get a clear picture of what you believe on a base, cellular level. It's important to note: It may not feel good to face those beliefs head-on. Maybe you too will want to puke in your mouth when you realize how far apart your reality and your beliefs are, like I did when I realized how much distance existed between how much I wanted to value myself and how much I actually did.

All the emotional sensations in your body are guided by belief. All behavior is a by-product of the sensations we feel within our bodies. When we are in a high vibrating state, feeling connected to our bodies, immersed in a deep, calming sense of self-love, we are going to treat ourselves and one another with love. In this state, we are going to go out of our way to make someone's day, we will fuel our body with nourishing food, and we will find ways to nourish our spirit and our soul.

And when we are in a low vibrating state, we feel lethargic, we are rooted in fear and doubt, and we feel small, incapable, and unworthy. In this state we are more likely to binge eat, skip our workouts, and throw hate at ourselves and at one another. In short: It's not great. But how did this become our reality? The reality of our lives is a result of our beliefs, thoughts, feelings, and actions.

There are five stages to the creation of a reality that you truly want to live in, and it all starts with belief. We can lay out these stages to see how we have arrived in the place that we are living now. I have found that it's always possible to trace our way back to exactly why things ended up the way they did—remember that there are no mistakes or coincidences. By naming the Five Stages of Creation, we can delve inside and reveal each step between our base-level beliefs and the reality of our lives.

Stage One: Belief

Belief is the invisible driving force of our lives, our motivation, and our reasons. This stage is the core understanding that we have of the world, and ultimately it is responsible for the reality that we experience. Our beliefs are shaped by our experience of the world we knew as a child, what we figured out growing up, and what we learned as adults. These beliefs aren't chosen, they simply are, although we can work to change them.

Stage Two: Thought

This is the noise that exists within our minds. It's the constant narration of our lives, generated through the lens of our beliefs. What we believe dictates the things we think on a day-to-day basis. These running thoughts reinforce our belief system and act as the default infrastructure for our feelings.

Stage Three: Feelings

Feelings are sensations within the body that are activated

by thoughts. The frequency of the sensation is directly related to the thought present within the mind. When we shift our beliefs, we change the thought, which changes our feelings and our emotional state.

Stage Four: Action

The action and behavior that we put into the world is essentially a function of our feelings. We are driven to do the things we do by the sensations we are experiencing and feeling. When we understand what we feel and can connect that feeling with our thoughts and underlying beliefs, we have so much more ability to control our actions.

Stage Five: Reality

Our overall reality—including the things and people we surround ourselves with, our quality of life, and our experiences—also stems from and is created by our beliefs. Reality is all of what you have attracted to you; all that you experience is a manifestation of what you believe about yourself.

When we apply the Five Stages of Creation nonjudgmentally and with an open mind, we move through life with a lot more awareness, taking full responsibility for how we are operating in life and, more specifically, for what we are creating and what we are destroying. When you begin to operate under the mind-set that "everything is happening for me in perfect timing," alongside the deep profound knowing that you can't control but you can influence whatever is in your experience, you will feel a deep sense not only of empowerment, but also fulfillment.

I can remember moving from force and willpower into attraction through creation and shifting beliefs.

I remember saying to myself a few years into this journey: *This is such bullshit. I'm so over this spiritual, hippy nonsense. There is no way I can make things happen through shifting my focus and beliefs.* I wanted to curse every spiritual teacher I had.

But there I was, learning these principles. I was being taught these lessons by all of my teachers simultaneously and they were all saying the same thing. It was as if the universe was no longer letting me get away with my own garbage anymore. I was being slapped with the truth on the regular, by multiple different teachers, all of whom I admired and respected deeply.

I always thought I knew better. I always thought I could force my way through any challenge—never mind that I was never successful for long. I finally had to come to the truth that, in fact, I didn't know better. And let me be clear: My mind and my ego didn't know better. My soul knew deep down, but I wasn't letting my soul speak because I was busy letting my mind run the show then. Whenever my soul tried to speak, I shoved that voice down, numbing her with food or perfectionism or control.

But I had finally been forced to my edge. Despite my commitment to making things hard, I let go and allowed myself to experience a new way of being. This way required work, but not the type of brute force I had so often applied to my problems. This new way of being took consistent commitment to the truth, to shifting beliefs in real time and giving myself unconditional forgiveness and kindness when I acted outside of my alignment. I worked hard, but here's the thing: I worked hard to make my life easy.

I don't believe in transformation through behavior changes. They are short-term solutions at best, and it leaves us in a state of constant frustration, warring internally without addressing the root beliefs. Does beginning with shifting your beliefs take longer? Yes, it certainly does. But over time, it is sustainable and unshakable as you begin to embody and live in alignment with your beliefs each day. Shift the belief and let the behaviors follow.

This is the path of personal empowerment: knowing that you are not only the creator, but you are also the destroyer. What can you destroy in your life today that isn't in alignment with who you know you are? What beliefs can you acknowledge that are keeping you distanced from the truest version of you? You are free to destroy the parts of you that no longer serve the version of you that wants to emerge. We are always destroying and re-creating, but it's important to do so intentionally.

There are brief moments when it feels like we have accessed the truest version of ourselves while meditating or on a vacation from the pressures of everyday life. In those instants of alignment, we set an intention to live as our highest selves all the time. And while we might get discouraged when we open our eyes or get on a plane to head home only to find the life that we have already built doesn't easily embrace our truest self with open arms, the key here is to gently remind ourselves that we create our opportunities to change from the inside out with feedback loops.

We enable feedback loops within our systems because of that direct link between thoughts and feelings. When we are in a downward spiral, we find all the reasons why this negative feeling is true, keeping us stuck there. The more we allow our minds to run, the more thoughts we allow, the more the sensations within the body intensify. But remember, here is the beautiful thing: This feedback loop is the same for high vibrations as well as low vibrations.

Again, we are the creators. We can shift this feedback loop into one of inspiration, love, and abundance—we just need to choose to do so. Knowing that we have the power to choose how we show up in each moment is an inspiring thought. Knowing that we can create the reality that we desire feels expansive and empowering.

Our desires are always leaving clues for us, showing us what our soul is seeking to express, how our spirit wants to be manifested. If you embody that desire, you also embody the inner tools to bring that desire into fruition. You have everything within you to bring all that you desire into the world and into reality.

INTEGRATIVE PRACTICE

Journaling: Self-Sabotage

When we don't allow ourselves to judge, but instead become curious about our actions and behaviors, our feelings, our thoughts, and beliefs, we open up so much space for self-inquiry, which can bring about personal and emotional transformation. When we allow ourselves to be open to the possibility of a deeper *why* behind the things we do, rather than jumping to a place of self-hatred, we can learn from our triggers and behaviors, rather than harming ourselves for them. We simply can't shame our way to happiness. It's a broken model that most of the world operates under, and it's time to work *with* our behaviors, not against them.

In your journal, choose three instances in the past when you've sabotaged your success, whether it was in a relationship, a health journey, or a new career. For each instance, answer the following questions:

1. When I "throw in the towel" and self-sabotage, what is the story I am making up in my head? How do I feel about myself when this happens?

2. What stops me from forgiving myself for the error and moving on?

3. What internal needs was I trying to meet by starting this healing journey?

4. What were my self-judgments?

5. When we move into a place of curiosity, we can understand the why of our behaviors and learn and grow from them.

For each moment of self-sabotage, ask yourself these questions:

1. The voice that was telling you to stop, that was telling you that you were already a failure, what was it afraid of?

2. What do you need to feel desired and inspired?

3. What do you need to drown out that voice in similar future situations?

Meditation: The Five Stages of Creation

Let's start by lying on our backs with knees bent to the sky or sitting in a comfortable position. You aren't writing the answers to these questions, you are simply asking yourself questions and allowing the answers to arise from within. This meditation may take some time, so make sure your body is comfortable but alert. Don't think too hard about any question that you ask, just take the first answer that arises and go with it. Let's reverse engineer the reality you wish to change. What is a current reality that you experience that you would like to change? What behaviors create your reality? How would you like those behaviors to be different? What are the emotions you feel right before you behave in a way you will come to regret later? What are the thoughts or self-talk that underlies this behavior? What is the belief that encourages this self-talk? Again, go with the first answer that comes along to each of these questions. Now forget everything you just did, wipe it right off the blackboard.

Next, think of a reality that you would rather have over the one you are living in. Sky's the limit—think about it like a wish you would ask of a genie. *What belief would I need to hold if I wanted to create this reality with love and not fear? What thoughts or self-talk would underlie that belief? What emotions would those thoughts and self-talk create in me? How would I feel if this loving self-talk was what I heard in my head? How would I behave if I felt these emotions as my baseline? When I wake up in the morning, I would feel . . . and then what would my behavior look like?* What does your reality look like? Really picture it. And how do you feel in your body inside that reality?

See, you have the opportunity to bring that feeling into your body at any time. It always exists within you. Whether you run this meditation backward for self-inquiry or forward for self-creation, you have a new set of tools for creating the reality you wish to see in the world.

CHAPTER 8

TAKING OFF
THE MASK

"You need to take off your everything-is-awesome mask," he said, looking me dead in the eyes.

"Fuck you, Philip McKernan," is what I wanted to say.

But in reality I sat silently in the middle of that workshop, mildly petrified. I knew he was right. For the first time in my life, I had been deeply and truly called out. In that moment, my walls crumbled around me and I was left struggling to rebuild them in an instant. I could feel 20 sets of eyes on me and a palpable tension. Day two of a seven-day retreat, how did he figure me out? At this point I'd been working as a health coach for five years, spoken on stages in many countries around the world, coached hundreds of women. I was becoming known as a food and body coach worldwide, giving others advice on their lives. I could feel my imposter syndrome ramping up as I realized this whole group of people knew my secret: the fact that I still didn't have my shit together. I felt like a complete fraud.

The truth is, back then I didn't know how to take off the mask and be vulnerable or how to express sadness—except to my mom. Sometimes the pain and exhaustion of trying to "be somebody" was so strenuous and overwhelming that I'd fly back home to Canada from wherever

I was in the world, break down, and cry in her arms for about three days, then return to the world and pretend everything was awesome again. I would take off my mask only for her. This was my classic pattern, repeated every three months.

The silence stretched on until, finally, Philip asked the group, "Who in here finds it hard to connect with Samantha?"

My stomach dropped as I saw the hands raise. About half the room. I swallowed and looked around. I've never felt so exposed in my entire life. I've never felt so seen. I had flown across the world to Ireland to work with one of the best coaches on uncovering your authentic self and now that I was there, all I wanted to do was run out of the room. I wanted to catch the first flight back to California, back where people accepted me as an authority on the subject of self-improvement and I didn't have to look any deeper into my own defenses.

But instead I took a deep breath. I stayed put and took in what this workshop had to offer me. If I was this bothered, I knew there was a lot of truth here.

"I want you to spend the rest of your time here being true to your authentic self, rather than acting how you think we want you to act," Philip said. "Act as you are. Experience integrity between how you're feeling and how you're showing up to everyone. It will be one of the greatest challenges for you, but it may change everything."

When the session was over, I walked down the path to my little cottage. Feeling naked and raw, I was ready to consume every calorie I could get my hands on. I could feel the mist from the light rain dust my face as I walked down the cobblestone street. To my left was one of those cozy Irish pubs. It looked inviting and warm. I so badly wanted to bust through the doors and drink my body weight in Guinness and forget about what Philip said. I didn't, I'm proud to say, but I was triggered like hell.

When I recognize that I want to binge eat or have a drink or two to take the edge off, I question that feeling and ask myself why I am feeling that way. We all have triggers, reminders of pain and weakness that make us want to engage in a numbing behavior. When I'm triggered—which is essentially the feeling of stabbing knives in my gut and near unbearable anxiety—I punch pillows and scream at the top of my lungs. And when I've dulled some of those knives and released some of that anxiety, I ask myself this very simple question: *What about this is true?*

Triggers can be beautiful once we can find a way to sit in the discomfort of the emotional sensation they create and appreciate what they are trying to communicate. The true purpose and lesson of a trigger is to learn about ourselves and understand what within us still needs to be loved and healed. I went into my cottage, made myself a cup of tea, and sat in front of the fire. I pulled out my journal and started writing.

What about this is true?

I began the biggest brain dump in the history of brain dumps. I wrote and wrote until my hand was cramping and my tea was cold. Turns out there was quite a lot of truth wrapped up in that one little trigger. Philip nailed it, as much as I hated to admit it. As I wrapped up the workshop, I knew I had a lot of questions about how I presented myself to people and the world around me.

I crafted the everything-is-awesome mask as a little kid and never took it off. This mask was my shield, it was my protection. I started wearing it during my parents' divorce. I was four at the time. It's incredible how from such a young age you can still have crystal clear memories of moments of trauma. The final days of my parents living together were hellish. When I think about them then, I can still feel the instinct to run and hide in my limbs. I saw my parents fighting, I heard their screams, and I still remember my mom sleeping in my bed to avoid my dad.

I can remember the sound of the garage door opening and my dad's Cadillac screeching out of the driveway immediately after a particularly heated battle with my mom. I can remember her warm hands covering my ears to protect me. I felt her pain. I could see it in her face as my dad's car drove away. "Mommy, it's okay. Daddy will be back, everything is fine," I said.

You know that pull you have deep inside, the feeling of so desperately wanting to take the pain away of someone you love? I learned this feeling at four and never lost it. I so desperately wanted to take on her pain as my own, to vanquish her hurt. As soon as the final word of the fight was spoken, Mom would crawl into my bed and I'd assure her everything was going to be great. I tried my hardest to convince her as I saw the tears roll down her face.

From that young age until I was nearly 30 I used my everything-is-awesome mask as a coping mechanism. Not only did I wear this mask to protect myself from the outside world, I used it to protect myself from my inside world and it allowed me to be in denial of my feelings. I was trying to convince the world, and myself, that everything was awesome. It rarely was.

You might be barely holding it together inside from the shame of your 56th failed diet, or the almost physical pain you feel when you look into the mirror and remember how much you hate your body—but in the next breath, when someone you care about asks you how you are doing, you say that you're "great." And you smile. That is your everything-is-awesome mask. When you post the polished version of your life on Instagram and hide the truth from loved ones to try and save face, hiding the reality of what is really going on, that is your everything-is-awesome mask, too. Why do we do this? Why do we hide our truest expressions of what is real?

It's purely ego. Bless the ego—it can support us in some incredible things, but it's a bitch when we are in the process of transformation and healing. The only reason we edit and monitor our responses or wear these masks is because we are terrified that we won't be lovable to others in our raw, reckless, and emotional truth. We have internalized so many stories as individuals and as a culture that encourage us to conceal our true feelings—"it's weak to cry" and "fake it till you make it." These stories cause us to stay stuck in the same negative personal narrative, stuck in the suffering.

Imagine speaking the truth of how you actually feel on a regular basis, unafraid of judgment. Imagine answering with the truth each time someone asked you how you were or, rather than showing what you think people want to see, you showed people the truth of what is going on with you on the inside. How freeing would it be? How light would you feel, unburdened by shame and expectations?

Another benefit of speaking your emotions and removing that mask: It eliminates fake friends in a hurry. When we show people our truth, we allow them to love us anyway, but if they don't, just show them the door. The people around you are all at different places in their journey with self-love and self-acceptance as well, so they might not be ready for your truth. So maybe you reconnect when they have grown emotionally or maybe not, but once you have taken off that mask, don't put it back on for anyone. And here is the interesting thing: There were, and still are, times in my life when I am convinced I am the only nutcase experiencing the depth of perceived insanity and disconnection within my body. Then I remember I am among seven billion other humans who feel the same things. We might process and deal with these things differently, but the sensations remain.

Along your journey, have you ever felt like you are the only one going through what you are experiencing? Or have you felt like your pain was "way worse" than the next person's? This happens because most of us don't talk openly about how bad it can get and we don't talk openly about the real stuff that truly matters. We don't talk about food or body weight in a productive way. But imagine if we did. We would all feel a little less insane and be able to navigate this life with a little more ease. Think about the last time you had a conversation about your latest diet with a friend, or a "you're not fat, I'm fat" conversation, or any conversation about food and weight, for that matter. Have you ever had a real honest conversation that started with: "I am just trying to accept my body the way it is because I believe in my body's wisdom"?

As a culture it is not just food and body issues that we are in some serious denial about. We seem to be allergic to talking about anything that makes us feel slightly self-conscious. Imagine what it would be like to really open up about how messy we can actually feel on the inside.

I could tell you about the time I threw myself down the stairs because I wanted to feel something, anything other than anxiety, or the times I lied to avoid a social situation in which I thought I wouldn't be able to control my desire to overeat, or the times I couldn't even bring myself to get dressed after critiquing my own body in the bathroom mirror, convinced I was obese when actually I was underweight. All these painful moments in time when I thought I was the only one, isolated and strange. You might believe it still, that you are the only one out there struggling to love or accept yourself and the wisdom your body can offer you. But we are not alone in these experiences. You are not alone.

When we are young, we develop strategies to protect ourselves—as I did with my everything-is-awesome mask. We develop masks to protect our image or to protect ourselves from hurtful moments in our past that we don't want to experience again. The masks we wear make it so we don't have to deal with the truth and the emotions at hand. The most important thing we can do here is understand what masks we are wearing so we can move through them. I know this might feel terrifying or even impractical—after all, you relied on that mask to get through some tough times—but I promise you it is possible. We can take them off slowly, one by one, chipping away the very things that keep us stuck.

Masks come in all shapes and sizes. We can wear multiple masks simultaneously, and the majority of the time we are completely unaware of them. There are masks we hide behind to make others comfortable, but also masks to intimidate and scare others away. And there are masks we wear to make others feel pity for us and masks to make us invisible. The masks we wear are solely dependent on how we received love as a child, so this is the first place we want to look in order to make our masks visible to ourselves.

Ask yourself: *How did I try to receive love from Mom and Dad?* Perhaps early in life you found attention in being the victim of a sibling or schoolmate's cruelty, and you found that complaining to a parent or teacher helped you to get your needs met. Sometimes we carry these actions and beliefs into adulthood. We might believe we are always a victim, and so we wait for someone to come along to save us.

Even once you begin to recognize that this is unsustainable, that it doesn't actually get you the kind of attention, connection, or self-acceptance you are seeking, you still aren't sure how to let it go. The pattern is so deeply ingrained, the victim mask so firmly in place, that you can see you are driving people away from connecting with you as you tell the same sob stories and complain, but you don't know how to connect from a more authentic place. When you look in the mirror and see yourself, it's hard to distinguish between you and the mask.

In addition to my everything-is-awesome mask, I wore a people-pleasing mask. For the love of God, this mask was a bitch to rip off, and to this day I still sometimes find that I have put it on again out of habit. I learned at a young age that if I bend to the will of others and do things their way while ignoring my own desires, then I will be loved and accepted. This worked for me for so long, I was under the illusion that I was accepted only when putting my needs last and everyone else's needs first. As a young child, my mom would always say, in her gracious, loving voice, "Samantha, make sure you always put others before you, make sure you take care of everyone. That is the polite thing to do." Boy, did I ever take that to heart. Even in the depths of my diet depression, the days when getting out of bed was a struggle, I still would be there in an instant if one of my friends needed me, but showing up for myself was an impossible task. But piece by piece the people-pleasing mask is coming off and I have never felt freer.

I want to make an important distinction here: there is a difference between habitual people-pleasing and being a helpful, supportive, generous person. People-pleasing is doing things to be loved; it's overextending yourself because you are afraid of not being accepted. It's saying yes when you mean no and saying no when you mean yes, and it always sparks resentment.

This people-pleasing mask often feels particularly glued on for women. Not so long ago, I was geeking out reading *Elephant Journal*, and I read that back in tribal times if a woman was not accepted into the tribe, she would be ostracized and die. We are ultimately social animals, and a lack of acceptance into the tribe means—to the primordial part of our brain—death. Therefore, we avoid it at all costs. We conform and layer on masks to protect us from judgment.

Of course, we need to remember we are working with brains that are hundreds of thousands of years in the making, even if we have memories that are only decades old. You remember the feeling of not being invited to a friend's birthday party as a kid? Isn't it the same feeling as being excluded from last month's girls' getaway? Or perhaps not being invited to a friend's wedding when you thought you were close? I don't know about you, but I can feel it in my body as I write these words, that heavy and dense feeling in my gut. This is the body's response to danger and the fear of death, of course. Not being invited to a party isn't going to kill you, but damn, does it ever feel that way sometimes. Maybe this is how women standing outside of the community felt back then, that deep fear and pain mixed with self-loathing.

But when we give in to this sensation and go all out to prevent it by saying that everything is fine or that we never really wanted to go anyway, we are severing the connection and intimacy we have with ourselves. Dismissing these real reactions to emotion clearly signals that we don't care, we aren't bothered by our own needs, and we would rather prioritize someone else's needs than honor our own. The compound effect of choosing others over yourself year after year is huge, and it creates a deep chasm between mind and soul.

This is where the breakdown within our bodies that we keep coming back to is rooted. This is the birthplace of our disconnection and numbness, where our eating disorders first began to form. We are at war with the very thing that is begging us to love it, begging us to come back. Reclaiming your body, creating deep intimacy with your soul, and truly listening to what you need at a cellular level are the ultimate acts of self-love. And you can't do them if other people's desires and comfort are always above your own on your to-do list.

It all comes down to the fact that we are all just looking to be loved. All our systems want to know is that we are seen, we are loved, and we are accepted. That is all we truly desire, and these are *absolutely valid desires*. We deserve to be seen, loved, and accepted—and we will be—or perhaps we already are and we just don't realize it.

I've jumped out of an airplane, run for my life in Morocco, and been drugged in nightclubs, but breaking the pattern of people-pleasing and taking off that mask was scarier than all of the above. It felt like a death. I thought I would be abandoned, which—for a girl who has her fair share of Daddy issues—is a terrifying idea. But when I gained the courage to start to speak my truth, set boundaries to protect my energy, and allow the word *no* to effortlessly come out of my mouth without it being followed up with a long diatribe about how sorry I am, something interesting started to happen.

I was flooded with so much appreciation for myself, a deep, fist-bumping love that was entirely my own. Feeling into my no, saying it with power, and not giving my reasons why felt so freeing. I gained back so much energy and time when I stopped doing things out of obligation or out of fear that I wouldn't be loved or accepted. I did things simply because they lit up my heart. The things I said yes to were a hell yes, and showing up with that energy made the entire experience incredible. And I gave the people around me permission to put themselves first as well. When I said no, it empowered them to say no back to me—and I love them always for that. It was incredible to know I can self-generate this positive vibrational feedback loop all on my own.

Giving people permission to choose their higher self is such a gift. It's such a gift to be the example of helping people break patterns that don't serve them. When you powerfully choose yourself, you allow others to do the same, and this is how we ultimately will help wake each other up.

After coaching thousands of people all over the world, I've identified patterns that keep people stuck on their transformational journey. One of the biggest ones is the struggle between wanting to be seen and the fear of being seen.

At our core, we so desperately want to be seen by the world. We want to shine and know that we are important.

But then in contrast to that, we feel deeply terrified of being rejected and we are terrified of being seen, even of seeing ourselves. We are afraid of what we will find, if we will even like the version of ourselves that is unearthed when we are truly honest about who we are.

It felt safe for me to wear my masks because if someone rejected me, they weren't rejecting my true self, they were rejecting the fake masks I created to keep myself safe. And although this meant the mask stood in between me and true connection, it felt safer.

At the Philip McKernan workshop in Ireland, I had arrived thinking *I've got this*, and immediately found that I had more work to do. As soon as I had been called out in that workshop, I knew I would have to drop my every-thing-is-awesome mask and that I would have to drop all my other masks, too. Once I dropped all of those masks I would have no choice but to be my genuine, authentic self. And who even was that?

I realized suddenly that I was terrified of that prospect. *What if I don't actually like who I am? What if my true self is boring? What if my true self sucks? What if all she wants to do is drink tea or meditate? What if she wants me to stop shaving my armpits and wearing deodorant?* It sounds ridiculous, but I began to overdramatize this whole "finding my true self" journey in my head because my old friend fear had come to the party.

As I walked to the next session, the gray clouds swirled over the Irish bay, the scent of sea salt was refreshing, and it felt like home. I opened the door to the session room and found a seat. I reminded myself over and over again to "be real" and allow the mask to stay behind. I sat there feeling naked as hell but also feeling lighter than ever. I didn't realize how much energy it had been taking to pretend to be someone else, pretending to be happy. It was straight up exhausting.

Philip began the day's session talking about authenticity. I internally eye-rolled because everyone and their dog was talking about authenticity in personal development. It's like Personal Development 101: How can we feel better? Just be authentic! But as I listened to Philip talk, I understood that being authentic isn't about showing people how genuine and "real" you are, it's about getting to the truth of who you are, not who you *think* you are. Good God—had Philip read my journal? How did he know this is what I was so terrified of? I so badly wanted to facepalm and peace out, but I stayed, and I got wildly curious about the real Samantha Skelly. As Eminem would say, "Can the real Sam Skelly please stand up?" I wondered if I would even recognize her.

I sat there questioning my very existence, questioning everything in my life. *Do I really like tacos? Is that my true self?* Thank God that answer was yes—I wouldn't know who I was without my taco obsession.

Do I really like coaching women? Yes.

Do I really think it's important to find a man more successful than I am? Nope, turns out that's not my true self, just some arbitrary idea I had picked up somewhere along the way.

Do I really want to have the perfect body? Do I really like the group of friends I have been spending all my time with? What is it that I actually want for my life?

The exploration kept going and going, and I asked the hardest questions until I arrived at the final, most important question: *Am I happy?* The answer was no.

I could feel my jaw tighten as I received the truth of this. It felt debilitating. Happiness was basically my brand. How could it be that I was unhappy?

Through this highly uncomfortable process I began to realize that the core of my battle with food and my body was that I was so at war with who I was. My masked self and my true self were at odds, creating disconnection inside of me.

Here is the beautiful thing about being honest and taking off the masks and becoming who we really are: We become empowered by the truth. The pain of the initial realization is forgotten once we get to fully understand what feels good and who we truly are at a core level. We get to create who we are on the outside because we know who we are on the inside. We are the destroyers of all we are hiding behind, and we are also beautiful creators of what we truly want to be in the world. We can destroy all that does not belong and we can create what is perfectly aligned with our truest self, especially that collection of masks. And it gets better and better, because the more we understand who we are at the deepest level, the more we can create our life to be in alignment with that truth.

INTEGRATIVE PRACTICE

Journaling: The Masks You Wear

We all wear masks, and growth is about peeling them off and setting them aside one by one until you achieve the most authentic version of you, the version of you who doesn't need to hide. When we learn and we understand how to identify the parts of us that help us to hide from real intimacy, we can work to chip away at them, piece by piece. Without this awareness, we will be wearing these masks without understanding why we aren't achieving the things we truly desire in life.

In your journal, explore the masks that you're wearing for protection but ultimately are caging you in and distancing you from becoming who you truly are. Take some time with this. It may take up to an hour for you to do a brain dump of all the potential masks you might be wearing. Look at any behaviors, the ones that make you feel small, and ask yourself, *Is this my authentic self?* If not, figure out what mask you're wearing that is related to that particular behavior. Here are a few examples:

- **Everything-Is-Awesome Mask:** If you find yourself making sure everybody thinks you are the life of the party and the most fun, or that you are the most capable person on the planet, you may be wearing this mask.

- **Victim Mask:** If you often find yourself complaining that life is hard and it's not fair, blaming everyone but you for your failures, you may be wearing the victim mask.

- **Perfect-Servant Mask, or Perfect Friend/ Daughter/Mother/Sister/Wife/Co-worker:** This is the mask when you work really hard to be the perfect version of whatever you think your community members might want of you.

- **Closed-Book Mask:** If you keep your feelings and emotions close, never letting anyone get a read on you because you are convinced that no one would like the real you anyway, you might be wearing the closed-book mask.

This mask tells others to stay away, that you
don't want to connect, even if underneath it
all you do.

Write down all the masks you're wearing. Notice how
you show up in life and see if a mask is standing in the way
of your highest self, in charge of your actions. For each
mask, ask yourself:

1. How did I use that mask to try to protect
    myself in the past?

2. What are the fears of releasing this mask?

3. What is it costing me to hold on to this mask?

Meditation: Showing Up Without a Mask

Now that you have journaled about the masks that
you are wearing, I want you to really dig into removing
at least one of them during a meditation. I want you to
take a deep breath and settle into your body. Do a quick
body scan to greet and check in with your body and notice
your breathing, but do not make your breath deeper or
shallower. Simply pay attention to the rise and fall of
your chest and belly as you breathe normally. From your
journaling you know there are certain masks you wear as
self-protection. Imagine what this mask looks like to the
outside world. Is it a facial expression frozen in place or is
it something more abstract? When you visualize this mask
you are wearing, notice what happens to the sensations
in your body. Does your body expand or contract? Does it
give you a free feeling or a tight feeling? There are no right
or wrong answers. You will not be graded on your perfor-
mance; just notice the feelings you feel in your body and
label them without judgment.

Once you have been doing this practice for a while you might try to feel what it is like to let go of the mask entirely. Imagine simply removing the mask from your face and allowing it to fall to the ground or float up away from you. The mask does not have to be gone forever; this defense mechanism has done you a lot of service, so feel free to say thank you to the mask as you let it go. You do not have to say good-bye to it forever; this is simply a practice of letting go, it is just an experiment. What does your body feel like without this mask? Does your body tighten or expand? If feelings arise, simply note them without judgment. If you feel unsafe at any time, remember you can ask your body what it needs in this moment. If it says the mask, simply put the mask back in place. Eventually you will get to a place where you no longer need the mask, but don't rush it, there is plenty of time for this exercise and it takes the time it takes.

Each time you attempt these practices, try on a different mask that needs your attention and see what it feels like to let go of that mask. Remember to be gentle with yourself, express gratitude to your body for being in conversation with you, and give yourself the time you need.

CHAPTER 9

DISCOVERING INTUITION AND **SELF-LIBERATION**

I remember the very last time I binged. It was the day I finally realized, fully and completely, that binge eating no longer soothed my emotions. I was spooning peanut butter into my mouth, spoonful after spoonful, and it made no difference. No matter how much I ate, the ache of my guilt persisted and my pain only grew. My coping mechanism was failing me.

My body protested—my stomach stretching—and my mind was a swirl, but my heart was certain: I knew in that moment I couldn't go on like this. Everything in me rejected my old patterns and behaviors. I put down the spoon and focused on opening myself to feeling all the emotions I had been pushing down and numbing with food deeper than I ever had before. The idea of experiencing the full force of my emotions and being with my pain without coping mechanisms terrified me, but a subtle, quiet part of my body told me I was safe to feel, I was safe to feel all of it—and so I did. And in the exploration of my darkness, I found something that I'd lost: my light.

I realized that what I was doing to my body with food was hurting it more than soothing it. In that moment the truth was confirmed: I had everything I needed already inside of me. There was no vast chasm that needed to be filled with food or shrunken with hours of exercise. I didn't feel any stronger than I had the day before, or any more capable of coping with my pain, but on that day I stepped up to be with myself anyway, and every day since I just kept moving forward, one step after another.

I later learned what I was doing was a practice called self-liberation. The name speaks for itself: It means deeply feeling into the parts of you that have contracted—all your emotional blocks—so that you can release them and move through them. This process gave me certainty that I had the innate ability to move through some of these pains in my body, that I could heal them. I discovered that by experiencing my emotions consciously and fully, giving them all of my attention, and focusing all of my energy, I could begin to heal myself.

When I was triggered by something—a look in the mirror at an unflattering angle or a number on the scale— my mind would snap into action, convincing me that I needed a quick fix, basically anything that would numb or distract from the pain I was experiencing: inhaling a pint of ice cream, eating enough cheese and crackers for the whole party, or exercising to the point of injury or exhaustion. I would do just about anything to mute my anxiety and fear about my body. I was convinced I needed something external to make the pain go away. This voice was— and very often still is, all of these years later—present. It didn't go away. The only difference now is that I simply observe that worry, that anxious state, or that habitual thought without acting on its demands. Observing the mind while moving deep into the layers of the emotional body allows the mind to quiet to a soft whisper.

Self-liberation is knowing that within each moment we have the ability to alleviate our stress by observing our thoughts and emotions, without attaching our identities to those thoughts and emotions. As I mentioned earlier in this book: Though you may feel as if you have failed, you, yourself, are not a failure. You are you, separate from your failings and emotions. You are full of potential for self-liberation. This realization is an end to so much unnecessary suffering.

Each urge to binge eat is an invitation for us to come back into our bodies. When you feel that urge, dig into what is present and heal the painful energy as opposed to suppressing it with a coping mechanism. Every time you are feeling pulled into numbing with food, allow yourself to sit with the pain, anxiety, or discomfort just a little longer. Make friends with your negative emotions and hang out together just long enough for you to know that you are safe to feel what you are feeling and learn from it. This will allow you to realize that food isn't the cure for what ails you in that moment—it will only numb the body and push down the pain until it surfaces again.

That day, with that final spoonful of peanut butter, I realized that this process was, in fact, simple. Not simple as in it was easy or it didn't take focus or practice, but simple in that it felt right and natural. It was as if my body was like, *Finally, girl! Stop fighting and just be here.* Healing through feeling is so much easier than fighting the pain through numbing.

The pressure and self-judgment we place on ourselves are the biggest blockers of self-liberation. We simply can't be in a state of self-judgment and self-liberation simultaneously, so if we are judging ourselves, we won't be able to move into self-liberation. This is where the power of choice comes in: We get to choose how we respond. We get to choose to submit to fear, hate ourselves, and wonder

why we are still miserable—or we can choose self-liberation. We can slow down, feel the pain inside, and release it.

Your mind and ego won't be the gateway to healing.
You've tried that for years and look where it's gotten you.
Let's not shame the mind—it's a beautiful tool—we just
can't let it run wild. We need to program it effectively and,
once we do, our thoughts will be in alignment with our
beliefs, actions, and intuition.

This is the path of self-liberation: being highly intentional about acknowledging each trigger or feeling in
your body and what might be behind it, then consciously
choosing not to outsource the pain of that experience
to a pint of ice cream, a drink, or a crazy party, but to
learn from it. Be intentional about the process of noticing that emotional trigger, honoring the emotions around
it, and listening for what your body consciousness needs
from you to feel safe. Soon enough, you will have the ability to heal your emotional body in real time. You don't
need anyone or anything else. Everything you need exists
within you now.

I remember the day I first heard my intuition. It had
been there all along, but I'd been drowning it out with
the noise of my mind. I was 24 at the time and living in
a 500-square-foot apartment in Vancouver. I had pulled
all my money together to hire a life coach so she could
help me "sort my shit out." For months we worked on the
concept of meditation and intuition, both of which were
completely foreign to me at the time.

"So, let me get this straight. You want me to sit in
silence with my own thoughts, doing nothing for a mini-
mum of 20 minutes?"

For someone with a raging mind that is constantly spinning up new ideas and thoughts all day, this was a very, very tall order. But I showed up and I did it, day after day after day. I could observe my mind telling me how it was a waste of time, how I should get up and leave because nothing was ever going to work. But there was a deeper part of me that kept showing up, day after day. For months on end I showed up for my 20 minutes but didn't feel any of the positive effects that were promised. Meditation was awful. It was simply 20 straight minutes of feeling trapped within the confines of my own mind. There was no distraction—I just had to experience hell on earth, and, to top it off, pay someone to tell me to do it. But I knew listening to my fear was taking me in the opposite direction, so I stayed and showed up, even when it hurt like hell.

Thank God I didn't listen to my mind—I know for certain that if I had, I wouldn't be here writing this book for you, that's for sure. Fear is expensive, and in this case, it would have cost me everything.

After months of meditating daily and experiencing no change, only a game of ping-pong in my head with the thoughts darting all over the place, I finally felt something awaken within me. I was initially terrified because my first reaction was to wonder if I was pregnant—it was that literal an awakening! It felt light, it felt certain. I sat with it and gradually I felt my mind release the viselike grip it had on all the little stressors and concerns in my life. The deeper I felt into this awakening, the more my mind relaxed. I felt like I was dreaming as I allowed myself to go deeper and deeper into this state of calm and immense joy. It felt like just a few moments, but when I opened my eyes I realized I had been in that state for more than 90 minutes. I immediately called my coach. "I get it, I finally get it. I know what you're talking about now."

This became a game for me—being in my body and quieting down my mind. It was as if I had discovered a whole new world, one that was always there but just silenced by my mind. I began to play with this new guidance, asking it questions, being with it, allowing it to make decisions. I started off with micro-decisions to feel the visceral "yes" and "no" signals in my body. My own body—the one I had hated, stuffed, and starved—was blowing my mind. The very thing I projected my fear onto became the source of my healing. The punching bag for my insecurities and fear become a source of deep inner peace and infinite love.

Over the next few weeks I was completely in my own world. Nothing in the external world could excite me more than this power I had found in meditation, not even cravings for chocolate or chips. And something interesting arose from this practice: I began to realize this peaceful and intuitive part of me was accessible only when I was living in my body and listening to its messages. The moment I shifted into my mind—focusing on a specific worry or even a passing thought like, *Did I leave my hair straightener on?*—I lost access to my body, my intuition. I couldn't live in that place of fear and worry while accessing the deep well of truth I had discovered within myself. I could be observing my fear and thoughts, but the moment I attached onto them the well dried up and I was left numb. Just like our physical body can't be in two places at once, neither can our consciousness. Connecting to your intuition requires practice, focus, and time— but it's well worth the work for the clarity and ease it will bring to your life as you strengthen your relationship to that deep truth within your core. When you are acting in alignment with your highest self, you will find you have more time, not less.

Each month, I set aside time to do something called a life inventory where I ask myself, *What have I outgrown?* and journal. I make an appointment with myself—literally, in my calendar—to review my life, think strategically about what I am creating, and do some deep thinking about where I am going. When I first started this practice, I realized it was crazy that I had never taken the time to simply think about my life, think about where I am at and what is working versus what is no longer working. I obsessively thought about shit that didn't matter, but when it came to the thing that mattered the most, the path of my life, I glossed over it, never giving it the time or attention it deserved.

Humans are complex, dynamic creatures. We are unpredictable and highly unstable. This is the truth. Most of humanity is just barely keeping it together, running around trying to pay the bills, get food on the table, and get through life the best way they can. There is so much unnecessary suffering in the world because we lack self-awareness and access to our natural intuition. When you fail to prioritize these keys to your existence—claiming you "don't have time" or dismissing the work it takes to explore them as "self-indulgent"—you are doing yourself a disservice. Self-awareness and the tools to tap into your emotions and inner knowing connect you to your highest self, allowing you to flow through life with so much more ease.

At a recent life inventory session I was sitting on the porch of my friends' oceanfront home in San Diego. No one was home except for me. They have these tall chairs on their patio that overlook the ocean, so I hopped up on one with my journal and began my practice. When I got to the question, "What have I outgrown?" my hand couldn't stop writing. Here's the thing about this question: Normally I have high resistance to answering it because if I admit something to myself, then that means I'll have to take action and move on from the very thing I wrote down. And that is a lot to take on!

But on this particular day, I had no resistance. It all flowed right from my heart to my hand and into my journal. I held nothing back. The thought of letting each of these things go felt like I was creating space on my emotional landscape so I could breathe again. I looked at the list with complete lightness—only a shadow of fear—and I knew what I needed to do. I needed to shift and move things around so I could be in complete integrity with this new version of me. I glanced down at the list of things I'd outgrown and I could tell by the way my body reacted to it that I was tapped into the vein of truth. It was as if my future self had written a letter to me. My body was telling me all the things it was done with.

I read the the list aloud to help it sink in, my voice wobbling a little as I said the following words: "I have outgrown my addiction to exercise. I have outgrown using food as a drug. I have outgrown comparing myself to others. I have outgrown dieting. Fuck have I ever outgrown dieting! I have outgrown projecting all my fear onto my body. I have outgrown hating my body. I'm done, I'm so done."

My body knew it was time to release the shackles that had kept me guarded and addicted to suffering. My body knew, but my mind needed to catch up.

Have you ever felt that? When your mind is lost in the confusion, but your body knows?

The mind is the glorious land of the "but what ifs." We are always telling ourselves that holding on to our current reality is the best answer because "what if nothing better comes along?" My mind was lost in a land of "but what ifs" while my body stayed consistent with the truth. It knew better. I know I am fully in touch with my body and accessing my truth when I check in for an answer and there is absolutely no negotiation—the answer just arises within me and there are no "but what ifs."

That feeling I had that day with my journal, that absolute certainty—that was my intuition, living in my body.

INTEGRATIVE PRACTICE

One of the greatest gifts we can tap into as human beings is our intuition; it's the most accurate guide we have for this journey we call life, and it's the most underutilized. We outsource our power by trying to constantly think our way through life, rather than feel our way through life. When we can feel the difference between a visceral "yes" and a visceral "no," we have access to something so much deeper and more profound, and we can surrender the obsession with details and make decisive, intuitive decisions. Oftentimes when I make intuitive decisions, I think to myself, *I have no idea why I am making this choice, but I am excited to find out*. Life becomes a beautiful journey and exploration and discovery. When we surrender the demands and fears of the mind and start to live from our intuition, we allow life to be a beautiful ride.

Meditation: Discovering Visceral Intelligence

Find yourself in a quiet place. You can do this meditation lying down or sitting cross-legged on the floor, whatever feels best for you. Close your eyes and take some deep breaths. Ask yourself a definite yes question, like, *Is my name Samantha?* Feel the visceral response in your body. Then ask yourself a definite no question, like, *Was I born in England?* Feel for the response of your body. Keep asking these questions and go from one question to the other so you can get clear with how your body responds to each.

Be open to not feeling it right away. This meditation may take a few times for your body to feel into it; keep showing up and practicing. You've been disconnected from your intuition for most of your life. Coming back to it will take time and patience.

Journaling: Self-Liberation

For this practice, you'll want to keep your journal handy all day, as it will force you to think critically about what you are doing at every moment, rather than falling into your old habits of distracting yourself.

When, at any point in the day, you feel the need to soothe yourself using your normal tools—binge eating, overexercising, whatever it may be—before you do anything at all, reach for your journal. Write down what it is you want to do. And then, write down *why*. This is the part we all shy away from—we reach for the cookie so we don't have to feel the feeling.

Write it down. What are you feeling? What is it that you want to numb? The act of writing it down will force you to feel it, just for a little bit.

And now that you have, now that you've been with this feeling for as long as it took you to write it, what do you want to do now? If you still want a cookie, okay—there's no judgment here, and this doesn't happen overnight. But have you maybe seen that the cookie won't actually have any impact on this painful feeling? And that you have been feeling it this whole time, while you've been writing it down, and it has been okay? *You* have been okay.

CHAPTER 10

DOING THE WORK

One morning not so long ago—when I woke up to an inbox full of hate mail, death threats, and one woman saying she was going to smash my windows in—I knew I had rocked the boat with my latest YouTube video. They say not to read the comments when you're a content creator, but I couldn't resist. The video was called "The Negative Side of Body Positivity." And I was hated on for months after the release of this video by some of the leaders of the movement.

The intention behind the body-positivity movement is beautiful, empowering, and essential: women learning to love their bodies on a deep level. We need as many hands on deck as we can get in order to shift the conversation and help women to do this work. But there is a dark side. This body-love message is leaving some women feeling powerless, confused, and overflowing with questions: "But how do you expect me to love my body when I've spent years hating it? This feels impossible! And am I a failure now if I don't?" I know this because I was one of them: When I was beginning my recovery process, I looked at the Instagram models and shamed myself constantly because other women were better at loving themselves than I was. I said to myself, *They are much heavier than I am. Why can't I love myself the way they do?*

A recent poll of my audience revealed that 78 percent of women felt that the body-positivity movement made them feel bad for not loving their bodies, especially when they saw images online of heavy women embracing every inch of themselves.

Here is the truth: We can't go from a lifetime of hating our body to all of a sudden loving it. We don't have a reference for what that feels like or how to even feel that way. The idea is complicated and overwhelming, and the truth is, we need to allow ourselves to feel how we feel without judgment. Body love takes time and it's not as easy as me simply telling you to "love your body." I just don't believe we can immediately, truly love ourselves after a lifetime of hating our bodies. You can't simply flip a switch on a lifetime of cultural conditioning and negative messaging coming at you from all angles. We need to be okay with being in a state of discomfort with our bodies and accept every minute of being there as a step on our journey. We can't love ourselves without identifying what we hated in the first place, reaching acceptance, and then moving through our own processes.

I'm going to say this—and it might not be a popular opinion: It's perfectly fine to admit that you hate your body. It's perfectly fine to be in a space where you are on the path of love and acceptance, but to acknowledge you haven't magically gotten to the end overnight.

I know this sounds counterintuitive, but what matters most is how we feel about our bodies, not what we think, or wish we could think, or what social media tells us to think. There is a huge difference. If we try and change our thoughts—repeating over and over that we love our bodies, just hoping that saying it will make it so—without addressing what is really happening in our visceral, intuitive bodies, we will ultimately be taken over by the feelings of unworthiness that make up our true conception of ourselves.

I definitely believe the intentionality behind the body-positivity movement is incredible. But if you are beginning this journey—as most do—in a place of hatred and resentment for your physical self, then it will take some time to feel authentic love for your body. After coaching tens of thousands of women, and through my own personal journey, I can tell you one very important thing: You can't skip steps on your way to sustainable body love, and you need to be honest as hell with yourself on which stage you are in. It is simply not enough to think about body positivity passively; you are going to have to work it.

So let's talk about what I call the Four Stages of Body Love.

Stage One: Understand You Don't Hate Your Body

This first stage is about recognizing that you don't hate your body. You may hate what the fat represents on your body, but not the entirety of your body. Let's get one basic fact straight: Without your body you wouldn't be here reading this book. Perhaps you have a story that the fat on your body represents being unlovable, unworthy, or undesirable. Maybe you have a story about your body being out of control or lazy or unable to change. Whatever reasons you have for being at war with your body, whatever meaning you have attached to your body's shape and size, hear this now: Your body is a friend, not an enemy. As you will ultimately discover, your body has allowed you every amazing thing that you have ever experienced in your life.

Stage Two: Body Acceptance

Allow yourself to be okay with what is, knowing that you ultimately get to set the vision for how you want to feel in your body. Any feeling you desire is possible—and you will get there in a sustainable way, not through fear, restriction, or overexercising. But at the moment, you need to start by simply accepting where you are. There is no love without acceptance.

Stage Three: Body Neutrality

As I have said: You don't need to love your body right out of the gate. So often I see people putting pressure on themselves to love their body after years of hating it, and that just adds unnecessary pressure to the process of coming home to themselves. So in this step, we are moving from body hatred, to neutrality, then into body love. Body neutrality is beyond acceptance because you can accept something and still not like it. In this case, you're simply removing judgment. Your body simply *is*.

Stage Four: Path to Body Love

Once we master neutrality, where we no longer hate our bodies but we haven't yet landed in a place where we feel love for them, we can slowly begin the process of loving our bodies. Remember the time line for this process is much longer than what your mind will decide it should be; you can't set a schedule for love. This step will take the highest amount of patience and kindness, and it will not happen overnight.

Allow yourself to take as long as possible through these four stages, being in each stage fully before moving on to the next. Maybe right now your body feels like the scariest place to be, and that's okay. You are on your own path and, whether that journey is short or long, the fact that you are on it is beautiful and you should celebrate it.

◆ ◆ ◆

Once I was at a barbecue with some friends, many of whom I hadn't seen in years, and someone said to me: "Isn't it exhausting being so self-aware? Like I feel like you need to always question yourself and look at what is happening with your emotions. That sounds like a full-time job!"

I could totally see where he was coming from, and at the start of my body-love journey I might have agreed with him; it did feel a little mentally exhausting. However, as I have said before, when we do this work everything in life becomes so much easier. We are no longer fighting ourselves, but working with ourselves to ultimately achieve self-liberation. And I have learned that if I'm going to work hard at anything, it's this work of self-examination and self-discovery, because I know how much impact it has on my life.

Here's an excuse I hear all the time: "I don't have time for all this personal transformation work." It ranks high on the list of "things I want to shit all over." I love when people give this excuse at a live event to my face because, well, for a pretty levelheaded chick, I can get fierce as fuck in a hot minute. (I wrap the fierceness in a loving package, of course).

This particular limiting belief drives me crazy because it implies that in order to transform, we need to be on a mountaintop, far away from human concerns, dressed in a white robe sitting in lotus position. And that is simply a load of bullshit. This work happens alongside everything else you're doing in life. We get to integrate this work into every action, every breath. We get to be an embodiment of this work. We don't turn it off and on. We are the work, in each moment throughout our day. Not enough time will never be an excuse to not choose to show up and do this work, because if we don't take the time to focus on happiness, what are we even *doing* with our time?

Now I get it, most people can't knock out a four-hour morning routine that includes meditation, journaling, yoga, and whatever else. Some of you don't even have 20 minutes to spend on anything extra because your baby is screaming and reaching for your nipple as you are reading this. And here is the thing: Having a social media–worthy morning routine or buying all the crystals and herbs for that calming ritual doesn't matter half as much as showing up for this work in your everyday life.

I know one thing for certain, and on some level, you know it, too: Your commitment to managing the external chaos is a fight you will never win. We simply don't have the power to shape-shift the external world to fulfill our internal needs—that's just not how it works. We must meet those needs internally; then and only then will our perception of the external world shift and change. And that choice is where the magic starts.

We breathe 23,000 breaths a day. That is essentially 23,000 times we get to decide how we want to show up for ourselves. In each moment we have the choice to continue to be addicted to the struggle or to rise up and choose differently.

You are not your emotions. Your body is simply the vessel that is holding all the emotions within you. Your inner world is like the sea: The surface is only one aspect of the whole, and others can't see the vastness and the depths of your ocean on first glance. But you can dive beneath the surface and explore, observing the vast ecosystem within you. What if you were to choose to be only the observer of your emotions and stray thoughts, not attaching meaning to them—like schools of fish swimming by? What if you were to accept the feelings that are present, knowing that they are not attacks against you, but simply lessons offering themselves as opportunities for you to grow?

This was one of the biggest breakthroughs in my recovery process, this concept that everything is showing up for me. Each interaction, each moment, each feeling that I experience is delivering a beautiful lesson that I can learn from and dig into, should I choose to. This understanding freed me to be the most authentic version of me. I am not a by-product of my anxiety, nor of my emotions. I am me. This body is perfect and whole, no matter the number on the scale or on the tag of my jeans. I am the soul within it all. We can experience multiple emotions at the same time and each one has a divine lesson to teach. Increasing our bandwidth to feel these emotions increases our ability not only to heal them, but ultimately to come back to the self, the true self, the self that exists at the core of all the emotions.

We live in a world where body hate runs rampant— just watch a reality show or open a magazine. It's so much easier to hate our body than it is to uncover the tools on how to come back to it with love, ease, and intention. Misery loves company, so therefore we bond with our sisters on the whole concept of body hate.

How familiar is the phrase, "Ugh, I hate my body. I need to go on a diet"? It isn't an uncommon exchange between women, and if you by any chance have been living under a rock and you don't know what I mean, just listen in at any gym or yoga studio changeroom and you'll hear it. In a clothing store, you will hear women talking about their pants size and which of them is so lucky because she is one size smaller. A restaurant or coffee shop might have women talking about the fabulous new diet they are on or how completely disgusted they are with the 5 to 15 pounds they gained in the last week, month, or year. Body-hating self-talk is commonplace—most barely react at all when they hear people speaking so harshly about themselves. Or worse, they just respond, "OMG, me too!" We've been conditioned to hate our bodies at a young age and for years have been building and believing that story. Like so many, I was tied to hating my body, committed to the struggle: losing pounds, building the right muscle, and whittling myself down to that ideal body I had in my head. I thought the only way to change my body was to hate it into submission.

But our bodies are without a doubt the most impressive technology on the face of the earth—we can grow humans inside us, for goodness' sake! Your body can heal itself, physically and emotionally, if only you let it. And yours is the only one you have.

No matter which stage you are in, the most important thing to remind yourself as you're on this path of body love is that you can't shame yourself to love, nor can you hate your way to happiness. When we release the force, the effort, and the pushing, and relax into a more natural way of healing—which is slower and gentler, with self-love being the guiding light—we heal sustainably. The intention is to feel like home in your body. Your body gets to be that one place you settle into when you feel disconnected. Your body is always there for you, always willing to comfort the chaos of the mind.

What does it feel like to *actually* love your body, rather than convince your mind you love it? What does it feel like to accept it, even if you don't "like" it? What does it feel like to simply not feel anything about your body? And then, eventually, what does it feel like to truly, authentically love it?

No amount of convincing ourselves that we love our bodies will replace the work of actually moving toward establishing a loving relationship with our bodies from the inside out. No amount of posting #bodylove hashtags on Instagram will be able to viscerally shift our emotional systems to bring us to a place of complete body acceptance, neutrality, or love. We need to show up and do the work. It's *work*, but it is worth it. Your body is waiting for you.

INTEGRATIVE PRACTICE

Meditation: The Four Stages of Body Love

Living through and embodying each of these stages will take time. This is definitely not something that can be done through one meditation. But part of a journey is creating a road map, and this meditation will help you place little guideposts along your way.

Start with some deep, soothing breaths, getting yourself into a calm and relaxed state.

Stage One: For just a moment, allow yourself to think all the thoughts you spend every day trying to fend off. All the hatred you have for your body, allow yourself to feel it—just for a moment. But then, remind yourself that this hatred you feel, this true emotion, is not being aimed at its true object. You *do not* hate your body. You hate what fat represents on your body. These are not the same thing.

Stage Two: Now is the time to accept that you have fat on your body—or whatever else it may be that you hate about your body. We spend so much time fighting this, fighting our bodies. For one moment, release the fight, and simply accept your body the way it is.

Stage Three: When you have accepted your body just as it is, can you shift how you feel about it? I'm not asking you to go all the way to love. Just try and remove the judgment and the hate. Can you feel neutral? What does it feel like to have the fact of your body, but no emotion around it?

Stage Four: This is where things might get tough. Again, it's simply not possible to sit for 10 minutes and suddenly have moved from body hatred to #bodylove. But the purpose of this meditation is to help light your path to the place of truly loving your body. So rather than asking you to love your body, I'm asking you to imagine what it would feel like if you did. How would things be different? Imagine being in that place, in that frame of mind. Think about all the amazing things your body does for you.

The more you practice this meditation, the more your mind will get used to these stages of shifting into body love—and one day, you will authentically be there.

Journaling: Body Acceptance

Acceptance is the catalyst for transformation. This means accepting ourselves when all we want to do is avoid, hide, and ignore the pain. It takes courage to look with love at the parts of us we are ashamed of. It takes courage for us to settle into the reality of what is, rather than distracting ourselves with mindless activities (and mindless eating) in a desperate attempt to ignore the part of us that needs our attention. We can so easily avoid our physical body as well as our emotional body, but doing so will have negative impacts and inhibit our transformation into our highest selves. We need to feel in order to heal, and we need to look at the very thing that needs healing, internally or externally. In this practice, we are going to be doing a mirror exercise, coming face-to-face with the very thing we've been avoiding and shaming.

Allow a half hour or more for this exercise—don't rush it. It's incredibly important that you spend time with yourself and be kind when things come up as you move through this journey. Let me summarize first before walking you through the exercise. It might seem scary or uncomfortable at first, but I promise you it is worth it. You are going to sit naked in front of a mirror and practice self-love and body acceptance for a set length of time, not just once but once a week until you begin to see how incredibly beautiful and amazing your body truly is.

To start things off and allow it to be simple, set a timer for one to two minutes, strip down, sit your butt down in front of that mirror, and stay there. Once you are settled—I recommend crossed-legged if you can manage it—I want you to scan your body from the top of your head to your toes. Each time you move through this scan, notice the judgments you have on certain parts of your body. Don't criticize yourself for judging, just notice. When you meet a place on your body that creates a judgment in your mind, simply observe and whisper out loud, "I'm ready to love you." Eventually we will be able to work our way up to setting that timer for 10 minutes and stay in front of the mirror for the entire 10 minutes; however, it is better to start small and work your way up to a longer sit. If you feel yourself getting overwhelmed, focus on your heart and meet your eyes in the mirror. When you're finished, answer these questions in your journal:

1. What surprised you about this process?
2. What did you uncover or discover?
3. What was the most challenging part?
4. What did you learn?
5. What are some new beliefs you've created around your body?

CHAPTER 11

THE DEATH OF DIETING

"Ugh, I hate bagels," I said.

My boyfriend, Eric, who had been, up until I interrupted him, expressing his deep, profound love for bagels, squinted at me, the crease between his eyes deepening. He stared with not only confusion, but deep disappointment. He is a New Jersey native—the type who struggles to say words like *orange* and *water*—and I knew he was offended.

Then his expression changed to dawning realization and he said: "Ohhhh, I get it—you've never had an East Coast bagel! I'm not sure what kind of bagels they are serving up in Canada, but the second you bite into an East Coast bagel, you'll get it."

"No, I don't think that's it," I responded. "I hate the way bagels make me feel, right after I eat them, like I weigh a thousand pounds. Eating them makes me lethargic and depleted. *That's* why I hate bagels."

He shook his head, scoffing, but in that moment it hit me how far my journey with food had come. I took a step back and was shocked at how my relationship was slowly but surely healing.

Years before this conversation, I would have had a completely different response to my friend's ode to bagels. I would have thought only about how a bagel would be the perfect thing to numb what I was feeling and make me temporarily forget the emotions I was experiencing in that moment. Like a powerful drug, it did the job. Stuffing me so full that things went fuzzy and I could disconnect from my emotions. In those days of my diet depression, I experienced only immediate gratification; there was no regard to how the food was going to interact with my system later on, if I was sensitive to it, or whether my energy level would be affected by eating it. All I cared about was filling a need in the moment—food was my addiction, my drug of choice. The quick hits of pleasure and fullness always would come at a cost. Each time I binged, I would pay for those hours of fuzzy oblivion with my energy, not to mention the massive bag of guilt I would have to carry for the rest of the day.

I began to explain to Eric that now when I eat, I always think about how I will feel after: It's not about the moment, it's about how the food interacts with my body— that is how I judge if I like a food or not. It's less about the taste and more about how I feel. I realized in that moment the growth that I'd achieved: I was finally using food for health and hunger rather than for emotional reasons. I gave myself an internal high five.

"Walk me through that process," he said. "Give me an idea of what that is like. I like the idea of it, but I feel like when there is food in front of me, I give in to the moment. It's like I can't think of anything else. I feel like I'm nearly hypnotized by the food—as if it has this weird hold on me and I can't not eat it! What you're saying sounds incredible, but I feel like it's damn near impossible to do on a daily basis."

I knew the feeling he was describing all too well: the verge of a binge. When it feels like something outside of your control completely takes over the decision-making, reasonable part of your brain.

"I totally get it," I said to him as I finished my coffee. "The way people talk about heroin was the way I used to feel about food."

The most difficult part of having an unhealthy relationship with food is that every one of us needs food to survive. You can't just stop eating. You can't give it up to get clean. It's kind of a cruel joke. Learning to use food for health and hunger was a complicated journey, one that came with moments of feeling like I would never get there.

We can break down how and why we consume food using the Four Categories of Consumption: hunger, health, pleasure, and numbing. The first three come from a connected place, using choice and awareness to guide our decisions, while the last is from fear, from trying to escape the moment because it's far too painful to feel.

Category One: Hunger

This is when we viscerally feel the physical hunger cues within our bodies, the sensation of hunger that indicates to us that our body needs to be refueled. Knowing when you are hungry means staying connected to your body and responding to the sensations that mean your body needs refueling. When we restrict our caloric intake, we are essentially ignoring our body's wisdom in favor of our own agenda.

Category Two: Health

This is the kind of food we choose to fuel and nourish ourselves when our hunger response is activated. This is different for everyone based on their body and what foods work well with their system. Take the time to get to know your body and know what it needs. Seeing a doctor or a nutritionist or even a naturopath isn't a bad idea. More important, pay attention to your body's cues. Once you are tapped into the wisdom of your own body and make a practice of listening to your body, these cues will become pretty hard to ignore.

Category Three: Pleasure

Food is a beautiful thing. It's a social activity, and a delicious one at that. Human beings use our common need for food to enhance social connections, celebrate special moments, and connect with loved ones on a daily basis: think cake on your birthday or a traditional holiday meal of comfort foods. Consuming indulgent food is perfectly fine so long as it is coming from an intention of wanting to enhance the moment, rather than numb out. It is wonderful to celebrate with friends, and occasionally indulging can be joyful and a way to mark special moments. Denying yourself human connection around meal times—even everyday meals—will only end in disaster. Spend time really enjoying the food that you eat, whether with friends or even just in your own company. Make cooking and eating healthy foods a joyous practice.

Category Four: Numbing

When we numb with food, we are avoiding who we really are and what the universe has to teach us. When we feel emotional pain, many of us turn to food as a drug to numb our emotions. This is destructive to our emotional and physical bodies, but it isn't something we are going to stop overnight. Know that it will happen occasionally along the way, and when it does, the most important thing is to forgive ourselves and move on.

I always think back to one particular woman who attended one of my live events. Even though there was no Q&A scheduled, I couldn't help but get her a mic when I saw her hand raised just as I was wrapping up. She stood up powerfully, as if she had been waiting her entire life to recite this one question. "How do you know if you use food as a drug or have issues with food? If I just really love food, do I have a problem?"

"What's your name and your favorite taco?" I asked her. Before people share at my events, these are the two most important questions I need to know. I mean, clearly. We're talking about tacos here.

"Kelsey and fish taco."

Everyone laughed.

My response to brave fish-taco fan Kelsey was that it's never about what actions we take, but *why* we take them in the first place. It's about the energy and intention behind our behavior.

Let's use alcohol as an example here. We can use alcohol for pleasure—to enhance a moment—or we can use it for numbing—to shut off the moment. Maybe you're in a good, happy place—say in Italy with your partner at a beautiful restaurant on the edge of a cliff as the sun is setting—and the waiter comes over to offer you a glass of wine. Having a glass of wine feels so perfect in this moment. You are about to enhance the moment and connect with your partner in a way that feels intimate and nourishing. Or—on the other hand—if a string of late nights at work put strain on your relationship, leaving you feeling stressed, anxious, distracted, and overwhelmed, alcohol can feel like the perfect remedy to shut off the world and "take the edge off."

Notice the difference in the intention with this: pleasure versus numbing.

Now let's look at how we operate within that same model with food: You are at work, and it feels like you are drowning. It feels like the weight of the world is pressing down on you. In each moment your inner critic is whispering nasty, painful lies into your ear—telling you that you are a fraud and you are a failure. You push through the day wearing your everything-is-awesome mask—or maybe the more accessible everything-is-okay mask—because you can't show your weakness here at work without consequences. When the clock strikes 5 P.M., you pack up your things and race home, stopping off at the grocery store on your way to stock up on your favorite bingeable foods to take away the emotional edge and to numb away those negative thoughts and feelings.

The intention behind consumption here of course is to numb, to disconnect, and to shut off the world. When numbing is our intention, we are operating from fear, we are operating from our inner child who is desperate to feel anything except pain. In this case, we are using food as a drug. After all, food is the most readily available and socially acceptable drug on the planet.

That false sense of ease will last all of a few moments before the onset of guilt and shame will roll in. Then the storm really begins. You can't seem to fill the bottomless pit, no matter how much you eat, so you still end up feeling empty—except now you will be overwhelmed with an even more negative emotion to start the cycle again. Not to mention you will likely have a stomachache and a sugar crash to look forward to, leaving you tired, foggy, and even more vulnerable.

I have this guideline in my life called the "20 percent enhancer." At various times during my day, I ask myself:

What would make this moment 20 percent more enjoyable, nourishing, fun, or joyful? Sometimes that could be lighting my favorite candle, turning on my diffuser with its lovely puffs of scent, putting on my favorite Spotify playlist, calling a friend to connect, moving my body in a way that feels good, breathwork, watching comedy—within each moment there is always something we can change to make things 20 percent better. Sometimes the 20 percent answer is actually food, consuming something delicious that will enhance the moment, like getting ice cream with a friend after a walk together, or a fancy meal to mark a special occasion. This choice comes from presence and awareness, not from fear or the desire for numbing oblivion. When I choose food in moments like these, I am operating from a connected place in my body, and looking to enhance an already pleasant moment, not blot it out. See the difference there?

The massive mental shift I needed to make in order to forgo bagels *and* still treat myself from time to time came down to one very simple but challenging principle: I needed to value my future self more. And when I say "future self," that can mean the version of me 10 minutes from now or 10 years from now. But this future self is not the one with the stomachache from eating a whole pint of ice cream five minutes post-binge, or still struggling with her weight and self-image years from now. The future self is the version of us that we aspire to be, or the version of us that is our truth, not our conditioning and who others said we should be.

I needed to adapt a new mentality of long-term positivity, to become someone today that my future self would be proud of. I called this version my higher self. I mapped out who she was, how she felt, what her energy was on a daily basis, how present she was, how deeply she loved.

Most people in my life call me Sam or Skelly, so my higher self was Samantha, which felt a lot more royal and mature. I allowed Samantha to come in when I was in the midst of nearly falling victim to my fears and limitations, in the midst of temptation to use food as a drug. When I invite Samantha in, *she* gets to make the decisions.

When I think about eating something, I ask myself if it's in alignment with how Samantha wants to feel—is the desire to eat coming from a place of hunger, health, pleasure, or numbing? Even just the simple process of asking this question is powerful—it brings me directly into the present moment and allows me to drop mental obsessions and be present within my body. It's impossible to binge eat when we are fully present. Binge eating is a symptom of fear, obsession, and being overly consumed mentally, while being present and embodied allows us to understand and feel our visceral intelligence, the part of us that is always speaking truth. When we are here and our bodies make the decisions for us, we are always guided into actions that are best for us, bringing us closer and closer to our highest selves.

In order to transform, we need to start with the outcome in mind. What is the most ideal outcome you desire from this journey with your body? When you imagine yourself in your healthiest and most vibrant state, what does that look like? Who do you become? How do you feel? How can you step into that version of you now, so you can wake up your conscious mind and allow the energy to guide you? This is a game changer when it comes to transformation. It allows us to release the motivation from fear and allows us to step into a place of acceptance and love. Not only will this journey be more enjoyable, it will be sustainable.

This journey took consistent effort, but I made it, I am doing it, and it's possible. Not only can you grow immensely during this process, you will get to a place where your fight with food is over. You will reach a place where you can look at your naked body in the mirror and have a sense of peace. There is a future where you can be social without the worry and fear that you'll lose control, eat the wrong thing, and spiral into a binge.

All of this is possible, and all of it is accessible.

I can remember the day I was done as if it was yesterday. Done with the struggle, done with self-hatred, and done with dieting. I sat across from a close group of friends at our weekly Friday night dinner: Each Friday a group of my friends gathers to break bread and it's my favorite part of the week. I sat there with a lightness in my heart and a smile on my face, feeling connected to my friends and my body and the present moment.

Historically, any kind of social meal would be a mental minefield, a calculation of caloric intake and the rigorous exercise regime I needed to force myself through to make up for the Friday night indulgences. But that night I sat there immersed in the experience, extracting as much joy as possible from the present moment and feeling a deep steady feeling of inner peace. I felt alive simply by shifting my focus. I felt fulfilled. I felt myself again. In that moment I decided that I was no longer going to be a victim of the "when/then" game I created to keep myself stuck in the battle. My internal monologue went something like: *When I am at my goal weight, then I will be happy.* But in that moment, surrounded by friends, I was flooded with happiness and contentment, the very feelings I'd been searching for in the pursuit of dieting. I whispered to myself: "I've got you. We aren't going back."

After dinner, I watched the sunset from the balcony of my friend's home. I had my feet propped up on the railing, and I took a deep breath in and out as the sky was turning bright shades of orange and pink. I noticed where my thoughts were in that moment. I noticed that they were not obsessing over the food I had consumed that day. They were not critiquing the parts of my body I could improve upon. They were not planning all the exercise I would need to do first thing in the morning. In fact, I was not consumed by any thought of needing to be anywhere else than right there in that moment. I felt peaceful, the kind of peace that floods your body to the point where you feel like you're dreaming, and yet you're fully present and awake.

I took a moment of gratitude to myself for allowing this to be. I thanked myself for the hours of work I had put in to free myself from the heavy chains and shackles that kept me locked, depressed, and in a state of extreme self- and body hatred. I know exactly what it feels like to be at war with your body and the exact sensations that creates, and since that moment on my friend's porch bathed in the light of a sunset, I know exactly what it feels like to be free and at peace.

Have you ever had those moments in life, when you decide that no matter what, you will never, ever go back? You draw a permanent line in the sand and you promise yourself that life will never again be the same. It was the moment that I decided to prioritize my mental health over my body image. The moment I decided to no longer be a prisoner to the number on the scale.

When I got home that night I threw away my scale. I actually walked the damn thing out to the trash can and chucked it in. I walked back into the house, picked up my phone, and deleted my calorie-counting apps. I think you probably know how intense it was to decide to throw out my security blankets, the tools by which I had been measuring my worth.

But I had decided. I was going to live each day with one question in mind. The driving question of my life would now be, *How can I love myself more in this moment?*

Previously, I had asked myself, *How can I lose more weight?* which of course drove me into a fear-based obsession that hijacked my happiness on a regular basis.

I was terrified when I made this shift, yet it felt like the most expansive decision I'd ever made. It was terrifying to throw away all my hiding-from-the-truth strategies and learn to truly feel my emotions. The old me, my inner critic, was terrified that I would gain a hundred pounds because I wasn't obsessing like crazy and controlling my every move. I made a decision to be okay with that voice in my head. I made the decision to be okay with gaining weight. After all, the thought of staying stuck there in a diet depression until the day I died made me sick to my stomach. Looking back, I didn't gain a pound. In fact, as my emotions around food lightened, so did my physical body.

Valuing my mental health over my body image was my greatest act of self-love. It taught me that my internal state was so much more valuable than controlling my external appearance. It allowed me to see myself in a whole new light. Now I wake up each day and I get to understand and love myself more, which then shifts my external world into a brighter, more enjoyable place.

We don't need to do a lot, bustle, or work really hard for it. We need to make micro-energetic shifts in our body to see these incredible results. Something as simple as choosing to bring more love into our hearts on a daily basis will have a massive impact on our lives. It will change the way we look at the world and change the way the world responds to us. Have you ever heard the saying, "The small hinge swings the large door?" This concept is incredibly relevant to shifting focus.

When I first speak to a client, I always ask a very simple question: "So, what do you want?" The response is often just a deer in the headlights, "I have no idea" kind of blankness. And when that happens, I find myself wondering, *So why are we working so hard? Why are we busting our asses in this life if we don't even know where we are going?* This is so typical of a dieter. We might hate where we are, but we have no idea what our ideal outcome is. We continually find ourselves acting from a place of fear, desperately wanting to get away from our current reality, but we don't have the end, or the outcome, in mind so we lose momentum and end up throwing in the towel.

There are two reasons for this. First, anytime we take action from a place of fear, we are doomed. Period. Taking action from a place of fear ensures that the journey is going to be tedious, with a lot mouthing off from our inner critics each time we "slip up" or don't follow the diet to a tee. Second, not having an outcome in mind is the greatest fail when it comes to personal development or improving any area of our lives. What we focus on expands and comes into form, so if we don't have that clear destination in mind, then we are blindly trying to get away from what we don't want without any idea where we are going—and we'll probably just stumble right back to where we started.

If, however, we begin with a clear feeling in our bodies of how we want to feel most of the time, finding a path to get there becomes a whole heck of a lot easier.

We live in a world where we are addicted to instant gratification. We have lost the true art of patience, of intentionally working toward something and allowing the results to come with time. We want everything and we want it yesterday, and that mind-set is no different when it comes to our health and the weight on our bodies. When we approach our bodies from this mentality, we burn out—we don't just burn out our bodies, we burn out our self-love.

But here is the thing. After years of programming your mind and body into a place where you use food as a drug and you are disconnected from your body, it takes time, patience, and kindness for you to come back home to yourself and be in a body that makes you feel peaceful. It takes small internal shifts each and every day, and it takes incredible commitment to our higher self. But in time, you will see external shifts that truly match the internal.

In Japan there is a concept called kaizen, which translates to "continual improvement daily." Being committed to making micro-shifts and changes to improve and become the best versions of ourselves is essential to this teaching. It's not the all-or-nothing mentality. It's not the way where you try everything you can—cycling through the latest fad diets and "miracle fat burners"—holding on for dear life and hoping for the best. It's choosing one thing each day to work on, to focus on, and to improve.

Kaizen requires commitment at the highest level. It requires a vision for something greater and a clear outcome of where we are going. Sound familiar? I am talking about commitment to your higher self—your version of my Samantha—the part of you that is rooting you on no matter how many times you fail. It's easy to get hyped up about the changes we want to maken in our lives when we read an inspiring new book, listen to a podcast, or attend an event, but what is essential is the micro-moments and micro-decisions we make every single day. These ultimately drive our success. Those big moments of inspiration and learning are important, but when they are not followed by a commitment each day, they are less and less useful.

When we are on the path to heal our relationship with food and our body, commitment is everything, but don't get it twisted: Commitment doesn't mean perfection. You can mess up, indulge, or even binge eat on this journey. The commitment you make is to come back to your center and urge yourself forward time and time again as you learn from your mistakes. Commitment isn't black and white. The path to sustainable transformation allows for us to be human. There is no getting away from that one: You are human and you make mistakes. In the long run, it will serve you to really embrace that. When we experience it all—the good, the bad, and the ugly—without judgment, knowing that we are committed to our higher selves and one bad moment doesn't mean we are back to square one, this process is not only so much easier, but so much more enjoyable.

We can get so tripped up by thinking we need to fix everything immediately. It's essential that we take this journey one step at a time, one day at a time, infusing kindness and compassion into each moment. And when we slip up, we need to give ourselves permission to be as kind as possible, loving the part of us that acted out of alignment with our higher selves. Remember, you are meeting and embracing parts of your body and soul that you've been at war with for years. You're meeting parts of you that have been abandoned and forgotten in your quest to be anything but who you are. It's not only essential but critical that you do this with love. This process of untangling all the parts of us we've created to keep us safe is slow. But it's worth it.

INTEGRATIVE PRACTICE

We so often operate from our conditioning. We base our decisions on the fears, masks, and insecurities that limit us from seeing, feeling, and reaching our potential. My wish for you, my love, is to spend all your time seeing the world through the eyes of your highest self, the version of you that is powerful, loving, and connected. The part of you that radiates queen energy from her being, the one who operates from love, not fear. I want you to have an intimate relationship with this part of you from now on: She will have a seat at the table, she will advise you on all your decisions and be the loving mother figure you may have missed growing up. She is your guiding force. When you're lost, look within to access the answer. She is always there for you.

Meditation: Discovering Your Highest Self

Sit in a comfortable position. Take a deep breath and do a simple body scan, beginning with your toes and moving up through your legs, torso, chest, arms, shoulders, neck, and face. Make a note of any comfort or discomfort, but do not judge it. If you notice that you get stuck on thoughts about one body part or another, simply note that those thoughts are there without labeling them positive or negative. Start to notice your breath as you move it in and out of your body. Do not change the breath or make it deeper. Just breathe. When you notice your mind wander, simply bring your attention back to your breath. Your mind will wander often at first, but simply remind it that right now your body is breathing and that is what you are paying attention to. When you notice that your mind has wandered, it may help to simply label the thought that your attention followed, whether it was planning, remembering, fantasy. . . . You might think of yourself as an anthropologist observing how a culture works or, even better, a biologist observing a tide pool. Simply note that thoughts sometimes happen and we can choose to observe them and redirect our attention to our breath. As you settle deeper into this meditation, begin to ask the question: Who is doing the noticing of my breath? Who is here to notice my thoughts? Who is here to observe without judgment?

Who is she? She is your highest self.

Journaling: Greeting Your Highest Self

When we start to realize that our thoughts and our comfort or discomfort are not who we are, we are greeting our highest self. As soon as you feel ready to greet her, try some of these journaling prompts. You might start with these simple questions:

1. Who was the person or energy that you felt observing your thoughts as you noticed your breath?

2. When I don't let judgment get in the way and I am simply observing my body and my thoughts, who is there to notice?

3. When I am simply noticing all the things that happen within my body and mind without attaching judgments about the thoughts or

the feelings, what is the feeling that I get about myself?

This process might take a while, so you might want to stay in this practice of simply greeting your highest self in your journal and asking questions about it for quite some time before moving on to the next journaling prompts. But once you feel ready, once you feel like you've had a firm handshake with your highest self, consider these questions:

1. What does your highest self truly want for you?

2. What does the energy of your highest self feel like in your body?

3. How does your highest self walk through the world?

4. What are your highest self's boundaries? What does your highest self say yes to?

5. What does your highest self say no to? Who does she choose to surround herself with?

6. How does she feel throughout her day?

7. How does she adore her body?

CHAPTER 12

INTUITION IS YOUR SUPERPOWER

I used to avoid uncertainty at all costs. I would create structures and rules that kept me in a constant state of predictability, in my relationships, career, finances, and—of course—my body and food. If I had a plan, I felt safe. And when things stayed predictable, I was able to relax. But this is life, and life rarely goes according to plan—and when things went off the rails, my anxiety would go into overdrive.

You know those moments when you carefully craft what you want to happen and the reality just blows up in your face? Those moments when no matter how hard you white-knuckle, life goes in the opposite direction? Those moments would send me reeling.

During my diet depression—back when my relationships with food and my body were the most broken—I would journal out my day, hour by hour. For four years, the day looked similar to this, with slight variations depending on what fad diet I was testing out:

- 5:30 A.M. – wake up
- 6:00 A.M. – work out
- 7:00 A.M. – shower, get ready

- 8:00 A.M. – eat breakfast (300 calories)
- 9:00 A.M. – start work
- 10:30 A.M. – eat snack (100 calories)
- Noon – eat lunch (300 calories)
- 1:00 P.M. – work out
- 3:00 P.M. – eat snack (100 calories)
- 6:00 P.M. – eat dinner (300 calories)
- 8:00 P.M. – drink slimming tea
- 9:00 P.M. – bed

This was my life, prescheduled, with my calories pre-decided. I was obsessed with certainty. I didn't know how to survive without it. I left no room to breathe, no room for the universe to infuse its magic. The certainty in my life felt safe, but it was strangling me. There were times when my biology would overcome my willpower, and I would end up binge eating thousands of calories worth of chocolate-covered almonds, only to have days when I didn't eat a morsel of food to "make up for it."

When we are addicted to certainty, we lose the ability to create, influence, and step into opportunity. We have to leave space for the magic of the universe to come through, and to step out of our own way, releasing the addiction to structure so we can create with the universe, not fight its flow. You will be so much more powerful and fulfilled when you step into the flow and let yourself be guided from within your body, not the confines of your mind. For us to transform at the deepest level, we need to understand that creating space to slow down, be still, and listen to the depth of our truth is essential—we can't unlock our intuition when we are addicted to certainty.

I was only able to feel a deep state of peace, freedom, and creation when I finally said, "Jesus, take the wheel," and gave over my control. Because the truth is, external safety is an illusion: No matter how much we plan, it's never guaranteed. Inner safety, on the other hand, is a state that can be cultivated by shifting our energy and focus and operating from a single principle: that everything is happening for you in perfect divine timing.

This sounds simple, and it is, but it's not easy. My path back home to my body was less a path and more a twisting, turning, roller-coaster track—the commitment to heal was there, but still there were moments when I felt like I was making zero progress. I rode the ups and downs and switchbacks and loop-de-loops for years, my only intention to be compassionate to myself during this journey back into my body.

I found that the way through this journey was to follow the guidance of my intuition.

At any point during our waking hours, we have what I call the Three Pillars of Connection: our thoughts, our emotions, and our intuition. The majority of us spend all our time within our thoughts and our emotions, but this is a disordered and unbalanced sense of reality, like a stool with two legs. Our logical mind is always trying to keep us safe—and it does a good job! But it can also overfunction, being so vigilant that it prevents us from living with our whole selves. Our logical mind is just doing what it thinks is best for us, but it often makes us feel threatened by non-threatening situations, and so we end up limping along, or just . . . well . . . stuck.

And our emotions don't necessarily help, either. You know the feeling when you find out someone doesn't like you? It feels like a punch in the gut. Your heart thinks you're in danger. Now let's be real, who gives a shit if Suzy likes you or not? That's her stuff, not yours. You will not be cast out of social reality just because Suzy doesn't like you. But it *feels* like you will. Your thoughts and emotions might be on high alert, but your intuition knows that this too shall pass and you are better off without Suzy.

When we can understand how to get to that place and how to quiet the mind and manage our emotions, we will at last have access to our intuition, which will bring us into a clearer understanding of ourselves and the world around us. But it's not always clear how to get there, so let's break it into digestible parts and revisit those Three Pillars of Connection.

Pillar One: Thoughts

This is our most active pillar of connection—it shouts at us, loud and clear. The cautious mind is always trying to keep us safe so it will make sure to show us all the things that might "kill us," though we aren't really in danger. Thoughts originate in the mind with logic, critical thought, and problem-solving.

Pillar Two: Emotions

We are flooded with emotions rapid-fire, constantly shifting and cycling all day from sadness to anxiety to happiness. Frequently we completely shut them out and let the mind run the show just to get through the day without the drama. But closing the door eventually leads to overwhelm as they build up on the other side, demanding to be let in. Our emotions are beautiful, and we need to understand what they are asking for and how we can best meet their needs— because if we truly listen, we can understand that we don't need to be afraid of their signals.

Pillar Three: Intuition

This is our true north. Once we can quiet down and manage the emotional and mental aspects of our body, we have access to our truth, which exists within our intuition. This place of deep inner knowing and body wisdom is always there for you, waiting to be felt and accessed.

Now let me be clear: Just because you follow your intuition doesn't mean your life is going to be rainbows and butterflies all the damn time. Your intuition will guide you to places, people, and situations that will help you develop skills and strength—but may not always be fun or easy. This may feel like you can't trust your intuition, but those very challenges your intuition leads you to are the ones that will help you grow and change in miraculous and beautiful ways.

All too often the logical mind hijacks the power of the intuition—making it impossible to clearly see and feel the path our intuition has set before us. We get so committed to understanding the *how*—how it all works, how each calorie eaten and burned will total up, how it will all come together—that we fail to see anything else. We are more committed to certainty than we are to the magic of uncertainty. We equate uncertainty with fear, assuming if we don't have it mapped out, we are going to lose it all. But fear is the ultimate diminisher, the enemy of intuition. If we ignore beautiful, powerful uncertainty, we cut ourselves off from feeling wonder or awe. If we knew all the answers, we would be without mystery or surprise. And anyway, life just doesn't work that way—there is always uncertainty. Uncertainty allows us to play. It allows us to create opportunities we never expected.

Tony Robbins says, "The quality of your life is in direct proportion to the amount of uncertainty you can comfortably deal with." This has been so true in my life. I also think of the time I spent $3,000 per month on a business coach when I was making only $2,500 per month. Most people would argue against what sounds like such a stupid move, but my intuition was screaming at me to do it—and as a result of that training, I went from making $30,000 a year to $300,000 in just 12 months.

Or I think of the time my intuition screamed at me to sell everything and move to San Diego. I had no idea where I was going to live or how it was all going to work out, but every cell in my body was telling me the place I needed to be was San Diego, so I packed up my car and drove 1,000 miles across the country. The whole time, my logical mind was questioning my decision, trying to convince me to turn around, play it safe, and my emotions were swinging from panicked worry to nervous excitement, but I had learned to listen to my intuition—and it turned out to be one of the best decisions of my life.

As soon as we tumble into uncertainty, whether it is by getting laid off from a job, ending a relationship, facing financial or emotional hardship, or losing someone meaningful in our lives, we have two choices available to us: 1. We can sink into fear and grasp at a safe, certain anchor—like pursuing a career we hate for a higher salary because taking a chance on our passion might not pay the bills—or 2. We can reach toward uncertainty as a place for opportunity and creativity by quitting that unfulfilling job to take a chance doing something that fills us with joy. When we let go of our plan—whether by choice or because the universe has knocked us for a loop—instead of grasping and fumbling for a handhold, we can choose to float into the unknown and surrender. We work so hard to avoid uncertainty that we cling to the things that aren't meant for us.

If we trust the whispers of our intuition, it can help us look at the situation through the lens of opportunity and possibility. What if we were to embrace that unexpectedly blank canvas for the gift that it is and say, "Wow, I am so excited to see the final creation"? How would you feel with the magic of possibility flowing through you?

Think about the time you let go of a diet that was making you miserable and you didn't jump into a new one right away. I'm pretty sure your emotions went into a tailspin and your mind freaked out, filling you with thoughts like: *What am I going to do? How will I keep control over my body? What if I gain 100 pounds? What if I put on weight and no one loves me anymore?* Our minds default to creating fear-based solutions to keep us safe when we don't know what's coming.

If you're going to create a "what if" scenario, why not consciously do so from a place of possibility, opportunity, and creativity? Replace those frantic thoughts and overflowing emotions with reactions based in your intuition and ask: *What if I release these habits that are keeping me caged and frustrated? What if I land in a place where my body's wisdom is realized and I can follow the inner guidance of my heart? What if all the stress of trying to control everything dissipates, and I can finally live in a more peaceful and loving place? What if I let go of dieting and become healthier, stronger, and fall in love with my body?*

This is the power of using possibility, opportunity, and creativity with uncertainty. It allows the intuition to create, rather than letting the mind and emotions infuse our future with fear and limitation. I call this intuitive decision-making; it is a process by which your intuition leads you to your inner truth.

Intuitive decision-making is about understanding the visceral "yes" and "no" in the body, and then following it with all you've got, even when it doesn't make any sense. And often—at least in my experience—it really doesn't make sense. My mantra as I make these decisions is "I can't wait to see why this is for me," and it's been my saving grace. Each time I've followed that feeling and made a decision without knowing what will come next, the most magical and divine things have been gifted to me. It's like the universe is saying, "Thanks for trusting me, Samantha. Here is the gift of your trust."

Is it scary? Yes. Is it worth it? Definitely.

Take a moment with me here and let's get playful about connecting to our intuition.

A visceral "yes" in the body is a feeling of inner expansion. There is a light, free, and excited essence to this feeling. Go ahead and feel that now. Next, feel a visceral "no." It's that super clear no that you get when you absolutely know something isn't right for you. Go ahead and feel that now. Play with going back and forth between the two. Reawaken the body to this sensation and begin to feel it throughout the day with any small question you may have. Use this little tool with food and ask yourself: *Is this a good food choice for me?* We are way smarter when we don't use our brains. *Feel*, don't think.

Trust and intuition are like a peanut butter and jelly sandwich—they go together. Feel into your intuition, tap into your higher self, and ask questions, gather the data, take the action, and then *trust* with all you have. The more you live in this way, the more evidence you will collect that it's working, and you will be able to make so many more decisions from this place of deep connectedness and knowing.

Now, disclaimer: If you don't feel a darn thing, that's totally cool. Maybe, like me, you've been numbed out and disconnected for years, so it might take a little while to integrate back in your body. Remember to be compassionate with yourself, and allow the body to determine the time line, not the mind. When I began this journey, I would check out completely when people used to jam on about intuition. I had no connection. I would essentially evaporate from the conversation and never come back—because I just didn't get it. It didn't make sense. But hang in there with me and we will reclaim your intuition, because it's there, we just need to dust it off and turn it on.

I know that you want to put down your fighting sword and be in your body. But if you don't feel that inner power of intuition and trust and love, it might feel impossible, at least in the beginning. You might feel like if you stop willing yourself through life for even a single moment, all the plates you're spinning in the air will fall on the ground and you'll cut your feet on the shards. You might feel like the second you loosen your strict dieting rules you will immediately gain 300 pounds—trust me, I've felt that and been right there with you. I tried to think my way out of my eating disorder for as long as I could, until I was forced to surrender, put down the weapons that kept me caged, and finally begin the process of trusting the innate and wise power of intuition within me.

We focus so much on willpower, using our logical mind and operating from a problem-solving mentality, that we don't understand that there is a deeper source to pull from, a vein of power beneath our feet capable of supporting us with all we desire; we just need to feel into it and use it.

Willpower is sourced in the mind, while true power is sourced in the body, in our intuition. True power is infinite. It is the source of all our greatness—we just need to tap into it. Essentially, true power is the infinite source of love that exists within our bodies at all times. It is available to us when we release the stories, fears, and judgments we have built up about ourselves and about our bodies.

As you read the words in this book, there is within you a well of untapped power and potential, a well of energy that has the ability to fulfill you on the deepest possible levels. When you land in this place of intuition and connectedness you can stop the incessant search to fulfill the emptiness you believe is within. *There is no emptiness.* You've been conditioned to believe there is—by society, by fear, by the Diet Industrial Complex—so that you will continue to give away your power and continue to spend money on fulfilling your perceived emptiness.

You are full. You are running over with true power.

INTEGRATIVE PRACTICE

One of the most important things we need on our healing journey is the ability to understand how the different parts of us are communicating with each other—or if they are not communicating at all. Each sensation, thought, and feeling is divine data, letting us in on our truth. When we get all three of our pillars—thoughts, emotions, and intuition—connected with one another, we can access our true power.

Meditation: Listening for My Intuitive Voice

Find yourself a very quiet place for this one. Sit down, close your eyes, and take a few deep breaths. Check in and greet your body. Do a quick body scan. What does it feel like to be in your toes right now, your legs, your torso, your arms? Is there any discomfort? Where is the place in your body that feels most okay? Can you bring that feeling of okayness to the parts of your body that may be feeling some discomfort? Breathe into that feeling, using the breath to allow it to flow throughout your whole self.

Now that you have established trust within your body and mind, tune in to your Three Pillars of Connection. Which of your thoughts come from your logical mind? When they arise, quietly label them "thoughts." When emotions or emotional sensations arise, don't try to judge them or give them a story or a meaning, simply notice them and label them "emotions." You are not looking into the why of your emotions right now, you are simply listening for the different voices that arise within you. Next, quietly ask to hear from your intuitive voice. It might take time, and while you wait more logical thought, planning, fantasizing, or remembering might come up. Label these as "thoughts" or "emotions," and simply notice that they are within you. Eventually you will hear what is clearly your intuitive voice. It might be shy or it might be bold— listen for the quality and timbre of that voice. Listen for the way your intuition speaks to you, and ask it questions if you like. You might not have a great relationship with each other at first, particularly if you have been pushing it down for some time. Assure your intuition that you will do your best to listen and check in with it more often. Let it know that you are learning to trust it, and let it know that you are doing your best to be trustworthy.

Journaling: The Three Pillars of Connection

Now that you have meditated, continue to explore your Three Pillars of Connection through naming them and writing them down. Speak out loud about how they are communicating, and what their needs are. In your journal, answer the following questions:

1. What are my thoughts communicating to me?
2. What do they need?
3. What are my emotions communicating to me?
4. What do they need?
5. How does my intuition show up in my life? Is it through voice, sensation, or action?
6. How have I been listening to my intuition?
7. How have I been ignoring my intuition?

CHAPTER 13

FORGIVE YOURSELF

My journey into self-forgiveness was a rocky one. As a dieter, I was way more committed to my suffering than I was to my liberation. This was partly due to my upbringing. Growing up in the Christian Church, I can remember clearly Mom saying to me, "You'd better ask God to forgive you," whenever I broke a rule or sometimes for no reason at all. I believed I needed to literally beg forgiveness for simply existing, not just from God but from anyone, so of course I thought releasing the past *must* be harder than just a few spiritual practices.

I decided to start with forgiving others as a means of learning how to find self-forgiveness. My mom and I have always been close, and because of that I know deep in my bones that she wants the best for me. I know that when she said that I had better ask God for forgiveness, she was using the best tools she had available to her to help me make peace with my own actions.

But that conditioning—from society, from the church—still had an impact on me. I believed I wasn't enough, and because I wasn't enough—not strong enough, or good enough, or worthy enough to be loved—I had to punish myself by restricting my food, bingeing, and punishing myself with exercise.

It was very difficult to move past this. I had to let go of years of berating my body and numbing myself with food, and tell myself—just as I knew was the case for my mother—that I was just doing the best I could with the tools I had at the time. Could I forgive myself for putting myself through all of that? Well, it was a whole lot easier once I saw that my intention was always in the right place, and that it was just that I had a whole lot of shitty strategies to let go of.

Self-forgiveness is a powerful medicine. It's a potent remedy that allows you to honor yourself but also put down the burden of years of pain. You are free to let it go.

Don't get me wrong, forgiving yourself doesn't mean disconnecting and pretending that your destructive behaviors didn't happen. Forgiving yourself is choosing to love yourself despite the destructive behaviors and choices you've made. It's understanding that you had emotional needs that needed to be met—emptiness that felt so vast it needed to be filled and pain that felt so sharp it needed to be numbed—and that you were dealing with your situation in the only way you knew how: by abusing food. It's okay to come to terms with that. It's okay to love the part of you that didn't know any other way existed. That part of you needs your softness and loving care in order to continue forward on the path to healing.

The journey of self-forgiveness cleans up your past and claims your future, setting a new standard. You are a creative being; you just need to choose what you will create. So often we don't consciously choose, but are instead swayed by our peers and the views and beliefs of the world, which most of the time aren't our truth.

Claiming your future means coming to a peaceful place within yourself. It means committing each and every day to who you are becoming. Ask your highest self how she would show up to each situation you find yourself in. When you tap into your highest self, how easily does she forgive? Allow her essence to motivate you, and allow her to pull you into your truth, into a present where you and your highest self are one and the same.

We are so quick to call it a bad day when we have a binge, or when we don't go to the gym or do anything else we "should" do. Our entire day becomes a write-off, and we throw in the towel when we haven't acted according to the plan we had set out for ourselves at the beginning of the day. I can remember during my diet depression days, I would eat something outside of my chosen diet for that week first thing in the morning and because of that one "mistake," I would go nuts, bingeing the whole day. I had convinced myself that I had already messed up, so who cared if I just kept sliding down this slippery slope?

This is the classic all-or-nothing mentality—the same destructive mentality that doesn't allow for a lick of self-compassion. A day is made up of so many moments, and each moment holds the opportunity to shift and change. Within each moment there exists the potential to release the energy of shame and choose another frequency, a new way of being that allows for a different decision.

On the days when I "messed up"—eating a forbidden food from my diet of the week or sleeping in and missing my morning run—I gave up the whole day. I would focus entirely on going to bed so I could start over at square one when I woke up, ignoring all of those moments in between, those opportunities for change. The next day I would try harder, push more, and force further with no new perspective or lessons to carry through and inform my actions when inevitably I "messed up" again. When did we decide this was a good strategy for transformation? When did we decide that this all-or-nothing mentality was going to guide us into achieving our deepest desires and dreams?

Rather than thinking of it as a *bad day* or a *good day* in such black-and-white terms—arbitrarily blocking your life into 24-hour chunks—I recommend practicing the art of micro-decisions. Starting off with small decisions makes the game easy to win so you can build up the confidence to make larger decisions. And in the moments when you don't choose with your highest self in mind, forgive yourself quickly so you can move on and not let the energy of disappointment and shame make its way through your body. Use each decision, each moment, as an opportunity to shift your vibration higher.

Choose to forgive. It's easy to shame yourself—for many of us it's our automatic response to any negative feedback—but you owe yourself the hard work of forgiveness. Forgiveness at the deepest level is built on kindness, so give yourself the gift of your own kindness by choosing each day to forgive yourself and explore a deeper state of love within your body.

Forgiveness severs the cord between you and the behavior. It separates your innate self-worth from any destructive actions you may take. I have said it before and I will say it again: You are not the things you do. You did something that does not align with your values or what you want for yourself, but that does not make you weak or a failure or stupid or any of the other lies you hurl at yourself—it makes you human. You did something harmful to yourself or someone else, but you are not a harmful person.

Forgiveness allows space to see things clearly and learn. We can't learn when we are in a state of self-hatred, berating our bodies.

◆ ◆ ◆

Take a moment and think of all the labels you have placed on your body based on other people's beliefs: "You're the fat friend." "You're the wrong body type to be a dancer or an athlete." "Did you put on weight?" "You can't pull off this outfit with your lumpy tummy and that butt." "I can't believe you ate all of that! What a pig!"

These off-the-cuff comments are traumatizing, and the pain we experienced can linger in us for years and years. Perhaps as you read these words, you're unearthing from deep in your body some of the things you were told that you held on to without even realizing. Sometimes the words of others become part of our own self-talk, and in that case we don't just need to forgive the person who originally said them, we also need to do the work of forgiving ourselves for repeating the phrases to ourselves and for believing them.

This pattern of pain can't go on. It's high time to unearth those harmful beliefs that are lodged in your soul. Bring them to the surface so you can let them go and heal the wounds they left. You don't need them—you never did—and they are no longer yours to hold.

Give yourself grace in this process, because it isn't easy. Recalling the memory can be vivid and intense. Years of ignoring the issue, letting anger or resentment remain, has only allowed it to fester and create even more emotional intensity than it had at the time. The thing to remember as you are going through this forgiving process is that you are completely safe, you are held by the universe.

Here is the interesting thing about forgiveness, both for yourself and for other people: It doesn't make the action in question right. Sometimes people don't deserve to be forgiven based on what they did, and that's okay. But the truth is, *you* deserve to forgive them so you can release their hold on your body, your mind, and your spirit. Forgiveness allows you to move on untethered.

For each person you've not yet chosen to forgive, there is an invisible energetic cord attaching your energy system to theirs. That cord is moving negative energy back and forth from their body to yours, keeping you tied to them. Your resistance to forgiveness creates more of a bond with their toxic energy, giving it importance and influence over you. The greatest gift you can give yourself is to let it go, to sever that energetic connection so you can create space in your body to be full of the purity and potency of your own energy.

Speak to your mind with gentle compassion as you move through this process. Speak with intention to your inner child, letting her know it's safe to recall these experiences so you can let them go and move on. The intention here is to get to a place where you don't feel triggered when you think of the person or situation. The goal is to come to a place of completion, where you can extract the lessons without holding the heavy energy, like in meditation when you observe your emotions and let them pass, acknowledged but without impact.

Your process of forgiveness may be helped by remembering the phrases "hurt people hurt people" and "people rarely treat others worse than they treat themselves." The person who was cruel to you was probably so much harder on themselves. Think about a person you've been hurt by, and as you are consoling your inner child during your forgiveness practice, remember they too have an inner child—one who is likely in pain as well.

Take a moment with me here and visualize them in your mind. Notice the activation that happens in your body, and love the part of you that feels nervous or anxious. Console her and be with her. Now consider the inner child of the other person. Think about how much pain that little one is experiencing. Think about how much agony they are holding in their little bodies, knowing their adult treated another human with so much disgrace. One of the most powerful and courageous things we can do as humans is to intentionally love the people who have hurt us most, knowing the reason they hurt us is because they too are hurting.

Self-forgiveness and forgiveness of others will set you free. Compassion and kindness are the anchors to this process, and we simply can't heal without them. As you move through forgiveness, always be mindful of what comes after—the freedom and lightness you will achieve from the process of forgiveness is a beautiful gift waiting for you after you move through the sticky part.

✦ ✦ ✦

Becca had completed my coaching program and she was just starting out her coaching practice. We were on one of my retreats when she looked right at me and delivered this sucker punch: "You trigger the shit out of me," she said.

My heart sank as my inner people pleaser began to react to the comment. There was an awkward silence, and the moment before I was about to break it, she continued: "I love you, I admire you," she said, "but there is something about you that is showing me where I am not whole, where I am not choosing to love myself. I am excited to explore it and find out more."

My eyes welled up with tears as I understood what she was saying.

"You taught me that when people trigger me, there is a lesson there. Rather than making them wrong or projecting my hurt onto them, it's my responsibility to understand why they trigger me and do the work on myself to heal," she continued.

In that moment, I felt so proud to be this woman's teacher.

What if everyone could be like her? What if, rather than suffering and then projecting, we could do some self-inquiry and heal from the trigger—both in the moment or years later? What if we no longer made other people the villain and gave away our power, but learned to keep our power by taking 100 percent responsibility for our experiences and learning from them?

Think about the cruel words said to me about my weight. What if they were actually said to teach me something?

I once had a coach who said to me: "Assholes are your biggest teachers, the ones who trigger you the most have the most gifts to share with you."

That was a hard pill to swallow for me at the time—assholes are just assholes and we shouldn't listen to anything they say, right? You might be feeling the same. Trust me, girl, I resisted this truth for a long, long time. I resisted the pain of acknowledging assholes as my teachers. But when I came around to the truth of it, I learned that each trigger I had was a chance to find the parts of myself that still felt broken, to uncover the parts of me that needed acknowledgment.

There are indirect and direct teachers. An indirect teacher is someone who triggers you from afar—maybe you look at their social media and you immediately feel less than or not good enough, because they can afford to travel and buy beautiful clothes all while raising a family. When people trigger us in this way, they are showing us our unfilled potential; they are the light that is saying to us, "This is what you could have." But rather than doing self-inquiry and using it as evidence, we shut it down and create stories for them, saying things like, "They have it so easy because their husband pays for everything," or whatever kind of story you choose to create at the time.

You are giving away your power every time you do this. Each time you choose this route you are not giving yourself a chance to see the divinity within your own gifts. The single greatest tragedy of the human experience is untapped potential—the gifts that we fail to see, recognize, and bring into the world. Each time we have a triggering event, we are invited to tap into our gifts and learn something new about ourselves.

That jerk on the subway making an uninvited comment about the body of the woman standing next to you is an opportunity. You have a choice: You can take it as a trigger that makes you want to eat your weight in Kit Kat bars, or you can view it as a chance to make eye contact with that woman and ask her how her day is going. Without engaging with the triggering event at all, you have taken a stand against all the inner voices that tell you to take on other people's garbage, and in addition you have offered some kindness to someone who might need it. Right there in that moment you are tapping into your gifts.

There is value in understanding our triggers—they all bring us beautiful messages and gifts. And trust me, I get it, this shit is hard. Spending time with the feelings we want to run away from is quite possibly the worst activity of all time, I know. But if we do the work to change our relationship with our triggers, we can use them to grow, rather than allowing them to push us down into darkness.

Use your triggers—those sudden and painful reminders of your unhealed wounds and personal traumas—as opportunities for you to step deeply into self-inquiry and explore the parts of yourself that feel shut down, afraid, and rejected. Find the wounds that need forgiveness to heal them. Where there is a trigger, there is a chance to heal and forgive, or explore an untapped part of you. Allow your triggers to reveal a pathway to your strongest, most well-adjusted self. Stay open while your heart is breaking, get wildly curious, and allow yourself to receive the gifts that come with the pain.

INTEGRATIVE PRACTICE

Journaling: Looking into the Past

I love journaling on these questions about forgiveness and self-inquiry as soon as I move through a trigger, or even when I'm in the midst of it. Remember, you can be triggered and still stay wide open—in fact, keeping your heart open while it's breaking is an act of great courage. It might help to pretend your higher self is asking you the questions—allow her energy to support you in finding the answers.

This practice is about looking at your past and leaning into old behaviors, the things you did to get your needs met. This is about recalling the past and cutting cords with those behaviors. You are taking the lessons but releasing the shame and guilt. Ask yourself these questions and write the answers in your journal:

1. What are the biggest things I need to forgive myself for?

2. If the shame in my body could talk, what would it tell me?

3. What am I hiding from? What am I afraid to admit to myself or bring to the surface?

4. If I were to love this part of me unconditionally, what would that feel like?

5. What are these triggers teaching me? What is the lesson?

6. How can I best love myself right now?

Meditation: Self-Forgiveness in the Moment

For this practice, you will be exploring a new type of meditation incorporating mantras. Remember, not all meditation happens in ideal surroundings—you're not always on a cushion in a meditation studio, on a mountaintop, or on the beach in Bali. You need some meditations that will work for you in the middle of your regular everyday life, whether you're at your desk in the office, in the back of a cab, riding home on the subway, or in five stolen minutes while the kids are playing in the other room. Wherever you find yourself, you can practice the art of forgiveness and letting go.

You know those moments when as soon as you do something you label as "bad," you feel an immediate sense of regret or guilt that hangs heavy inside your body? Maybe it is a binge. Or maybe you're so angry with yourself that you take it out on the closest person to you. In these moments, we are given an opportunity to practice self-awareness and forgiveness—and this mantra meditation can help.

Start by taking a deep breath and notice where you are feeling your emotions in your body. Then simply recite one or a few of the following mantras, while paying close attention to your breath and feeling into your body:

- Although I sometimes find myself bingeing on food, I love and accept myself.

- Mistakes happen, and I forgive myself when I make mistakes.

- Although I sometimes feel out of control around food, I accept myself as I am.

- Mistakes happen, and I forgive myself when I make mistakes.

- Although I sometimes use food to numb my emotions, I love and accept myself.

- Mistakes happen, and I forgive myself when I make mistakes.

CHAPTER 14

HEALING EMOTIONAL EATING WITH BREATHWORK

I am going to start by telling you a story that is going to make you think I am fully out of my mind. But honestly, you might think that already. If you have made it this far into the book you know that I am a jump-in-with-both-feet kind of girl, and if that is nuts, I am absolutely okay with that. So here we go. It will surprise no one that as I found more and more interesting ideas about how to heal my relationship with my body, I went deeper and deeper into research mode. One day while reading about healing, I found an opportunity to go to Bali and stay with a family to visit a famous healing center, and my intuition lit up like a Christmas tree. I don't know if I even thought twice about it, I just listened to that deep resonate feeling in my chest and started looking up flights the very same day.

First, I want to assure you that the result of my crazy journey halfway across the globe to find myself is something you can do right in your house on any given Tuesday morning before the kids get up or before you brew your coffee. You can use the tool I am going to share with you before the meeting that you have been preparing for months, or even after that meeting went terribly and everyone in the room seemed to have it in for you specifically. What I am saying is, the thing that I had to go all the way to Bali to find is something that you can do anywhere, and you can start right at the end of this chapter. By now you know that I am willing to try lots of different things to find the thing that works, and once I find it I just can't shut up about it. And this one, my love, is one of the most significant healing tools I have found, so stick with me—you are in for a ride.

✦ ✦ ✦

I woke up one warm November morning to the sound of monkeys in the trees and the sun shining in through the curtains. Finally, I was in Bali, staying in the home of a generous family who had agreed to house seekers like myself. I was in paradise, but everything in my body felt tense. The jet lag was one thing, but beyond that I could smell the sweet aroma of Balinese pancakes being prepared in the kitchen just outside my room. And the scent of those lovely pancakes was making me incredibly nervous. For a split second I could actually enjoy the sweet moment of sustenance, but then my good old diet mind immediately wondered how many miles I'd need to run in order to burn off something as delicious as pancakes. Would I offend my host family if I turned them down? Fear of not being perfect by every standard walled me in.

I heard a little knock on the wooden door of my homestay and then a voice. "Samantha? Breakfast?" I agreed and made my way to the little table outside. A kind Balinese man served me the pancakes with some extra-strong coffee. I tried my best to enjoy them without guilt, aka my daily challenge to eat without feeling as though I was doing something to harm my body. I am embarrassed to admit that I pushed his generous gift around on my plate to make it look like I had eaten more.

I hopped on my scooter and made my way through the streets of Ubud to the healing center I had come to visit. I dodged the monkeys that darted across the street and felt a peaceful sort of foreboding as I walked into the center and saw a wide range of healing modalities. This has become the world's destination for Westerners to find themselves and heal from decades of emotional turmoil.

I walked up to the community board and saw a sign that said BREATHWORK, and the advertisement featured a man dressed in all white with his hands in a prayer position. It caught my eye immediately. *Breathwork? What does that even mean? Just breathing? But why?* And then my curiosity started nagging at me. *It can't mean just breathing, right?* I looked at the time and date to discover it started in approximately six minutes. *Now is as good a time as any to be curious,* I decided, and signed up at the front desk.

As I entered the room, Michael—the man from the flyer—bowed to me and acknowledged my presence. There were mats, pillows, and blankets; it looked like an adult sleepover. I tucked myself into the very back corner so I could remain hidden and under the radar.

"Anyone here for the first time?" he asked. I stalled, but when no one else raised their hand, so I slowly and sheepishly raised mine.

"You're in for a ride," he said, pointing me out. "You're in good hands. Just allow yourself to surrender."

Oh shit, I thought. *What have I done?*

Michael announced that we would breathe deeply into our chests and then release that breath in a continuous cycle. Since we would be lying on our backs, we were instructed to get a mat, blanket, or bolster to make ourselves comfortable. As he explained what to expect emotionally, I couldn't help but snicker to myself. I hadn't felt anything but numbness and anxiety for years—what would a breathing exercise change? But I took a deep breath and gathered the things I would need to make myself comfortable. We were told if we felt unsure at any time to raise a hand and one of the facilitators would come by.

I began to breathe with the pattern I heard all around me: in through the nose, out through the mouth. I could feel my body resisting the practice, but I decided to keep breathing as instructed despite the difficulty. At first it was fine. I had just started to get the hang of pushing through the difficulty, and then I began to shiver and my jaw started aching and I raised my hand for help.

Michael came over to my side, kneeled beside me, and stared into my eyes with his deep, connected presence. "I'm in pain, my chest—it's aching."

Michael nodded and said, "Let the breath do the work. The tension is completely normal. Breathe through it and you'll find ease on the other side."

I felt into the tension in my chest, the pain in my jaw, and listened to the room around me. My breathing began to settle into the rhythm of the music that was playing and the sound of the people breathing all around me. I found that I was able to keep up with the intense but continual in-and-out breathing. It was as if I wasn't even trying to breathe anymore—my body was doing the work. The shivering that had started became more of a shaking and I began to tingle and vibrate. My whole body was becoming awake, more alive.

And then after what seemed like a few minutes in, I felt myself begin to cry. Which I know is weird. To lie on the floor in a yoga studio and just by breathing along to some music to just, apropos of nothing, begin to cry. But it was too late to turn back, and I thought, *Well, I am in Bali for a reason*, and frankly this was too fascinating to get up and walk out on. Emotion deep in my body overtook me like a wave. My body, the one that I had stopped listening to so long ago, the one I felt I couldn't trust. My whole relationship with my body was so sad. The cry turned into a sob; the grief in me was deep and old and I could feel all of it in my chest and my belly, even in my limbs. Michael invited us to let out a sigh or a wail. And the deepest wail came out of me. I had no idea why I was crying but I had never felt anything more cathartic in my entire life.

And then Michael invited us to laugh, and it hit me that where I was and what I was doing in the presence of these strangers was funny, and I giggled. I could hear other people in the room laughing and I laughed at how ridiculous the whole thing was. Just a minute before we had all been crying and now we were laughing; it became hysterical. That deep, hard belly laugh gave way to a feeling of peace, and then the floodgates were open.

All the emotions that had been cooped up inside of me for years came out one by one. And I started to notice how each of these emotions had a specific feeling in my body. How I had been storing all my anxiety about binge eating in my jaw, and I had been carrying the emotional pain of restricting my food in my chest, and my worry that deep down I was unlovable in my belly. As these emotions rose up out of where I had been storing them, I felt them deeply and then I felt them release their grip on my mind—and everything was joyous and blissful or funny again.

After what felt like about 15 minutes of the most intense emotional roller coaster, the music ended and Michael instructed us to come back to our normal breath.

I lay there, palms facing the ceiling, and was so still. This was a kind of stillness I'd never in my life experienced—so present, so alive. I sat up and glanced at the clock and I realized we had been breathing together for three hours. I was in total shock. I hadn't noticed the time at all. Michael was thanking people for their presence and the work they had done with him that day. The session was over.

I brought my hands up to my chest and for the first time in my life I could feel the intensity of my heart. Peace flowed effortlessly through my body, and my mind was calm, quiet, and collected. I had no idea my body was able to feel the intensity of this lightness mixed with this strange sense of self-love. Not the kind of self-love advertised in magazines, but an intense overflowing of gratitude for my life and my body. This shit was deep, profound, and remarkable. People got up and began to leave the studio, but I didn't want to move; I just kept holding my body.

Michael came over to see how I was doing, and I looked at his deep blue eyes and asked, "What on God's green earth was that?"

"People call it different things: access to the divine, or connection to the universe. But my guess with you is you finally felt the depth of your own love."

My whole being grappled with this knowing. I could feel that he was right, and still my logical mind fought this truth. I was so conditioned to hustle for my worth that the notion of just loving myself—loving myself just as I am—was completely foreign to me. I just stared back at Michael, speechless.

He smiled with a deep sigh and gave me his hand to help me to my feet.

"Drink lots of water," he said, "and take care of yourself. I'll be around tomorrow if you have questions."

Questions? I felt like I needed Michael to literally piece together my new understanding of how life worked.

I made my way back to my homestay thinking I would write. When life doesn't make sense, and it often doesn't, I write to make sense of what I am thinking or feeling. Except this time there was no story I could make up about what I was feeling because my mind had no reference for what I had just experienced. And then I got very curious. I wrote a list of questions and I took them to Google.

For the next few hours I read everything I could about breathwork. I was obsessed with understanding what happened in my body. As I researched, I became more and more intrigued with this body of work. I dug deep, reading every last article and sending every leader and healer doing this work an e-mail. It seemed there were many different kinds of breathwork and the one I had engaged in was specific for clarity and healing as opposed to a more spiritual type of journey. I rewrote my list of questions in the back of my journal for Michael, closed my eyes, and fell into a sound sleep.

As I woke up the next day, I realized that my typical morning anxiety had lessened dramatically. I felt comfortable being inside my body and I didn't feel the need to run away or distract myself. It didn't even feel like work to remember to appreciate instead of punishing my body. I just felt nice. The scent of the morning pancakes didn't trigger any fear. I just lay there enjoying the feeling of being in my body with my senses awake and bringing me delightful information.

I got up and ate breakfast without guilt or fear. I just felt hungry and then amazingly quickly, I felt sated. Somehow, I felt more present. I was in awe of the fact that all my regular notions of the if-then model of worthiness usually dominating my thoughts were just absent. You know the model I am talking about, that old "if I can just lose 10 pounds, then I will be really at peace with myself" garbage. I had somehow just awakened without that conditional acceptance and into this new understanding of the unconditional self-love that I wasn't even aware I had until the day before.

I went back to the studio and found Michael. Michael embodied the kind of energy that as soon as you're in his presence there's a sense of grounding and healing. I felt safe asking him questions that might have made me feel stupid otherwise. He was like a breath of fresh air; I could ask him anything I wanted. Michael gave me his take on why breathwork works so well, how it makes the connection between the mind and body open and safe. How it accesses all the emotions we store in the body as a way of moving on with our lives and helps to release them.

I was smiling so much my face hurt. "Why doesn't every human on the planet know about this? It's the most powerful thing I've ever done."

He looked at me straight in the eyes and said, "Maybe you will be the one to tell them."

Everything shifted for me in that moment. I returned home from Bali with a new understanding of how to heal my body and how to help others heal their own bodies. From that moment on, I realized that breathwork was going to be a huge part of my purpose.

Suddenly I had the tools to heal. From then on when I felt triggered to binge on food to numb my emotions, I have used my breath to deal with that trigger. I had never felt personal power like that before. It was as if I was given a key to unlock my inner calm and innate sense of worthiness. All this time it existed within me. I no longer felt dependent on external sources to access love and worthiness. Everything I needed to heal my relationship with my body was already inside me.

The reason why I developed such an unhealthy relationship with food and with my body was because I was fundamentally disconnected from the innate intelligence that lives within my system. The very act of dieting blocked my ability to listen to my body and it made me resistant to the sensations that were communicating with me. Dieting taught me that I couldn't trust my body to tell me what it needed.

The other side of that was that when I felt something I couldn't deal with, my body would take over, demanding food that it had been denied and that felt so good that I would use it to numb any emotion I felt I couldn't deal with. Breathwork taught me that I could breathe through any emotion. Becoming connected to my body through my breath showed me that whatever emotion came up in me, I could handle it. All I needed was to breathe into my body and stay present to the sensations I felt.

When we are deeply connected to our bodies, we become present to the emotions that arise within us and notice that they will all pass into other emotions. All of the emotions we aren't looking to numb become divine data; they become sensations that we are safe to feel. When we are connected to our bodies, when we feel safe inside our bodies, we do not need to numb them out—we simply want to heal.

After coaching more than tens of thousands of people in my career, I have found that there are three common answers to the question, "How do you want to feel?" The answers are a desired to feel loved, accepted, or connected. We are simple beings, really—it's quite simple to identify how we want to feel. But we complicate the process of feeling those emotions, making it so hard for us to achieve the very feelings we crave. I am fascinated with studying human behavior and potential because we are fascinating creatures. Why do we do anything in this life? The answers are almost always because we want to feel worthy, important, seen, and loved.

We set the bars so high, putting unrealistic expectations on ourselves and chasing things we don't even want, all in the name of love. It's not about the "thing" we are doing, it's about the feeling we think that thing will bring us. The career you hate? You stay stuck because you're doing it to prove something to someone who made you feel less than, so you can feel accepted. The relationship that is eating your soul and making you miserable? You stay because you fear losing love even though it's not real love. The friend who is toxic? You stay connected because you are so afraid of being alone, even if it's unhealthy.

Here is the beautiful thing: At our core we are all worthy of love and acceptance, and deep down we already know this, despite anything else we may be telling ourselves. The more connected we become to that innate worthiness the more love gets drawn into our lives. Within you now, as you read these words, is everything you need to feel better. You have infinite access to all the love, acceptance, and connection you could ever need. You just need something to shake you from the pattern you have been stuck in.

It's true that you may have open wounds left over from growing up, echoing messages or unaddressed pain from when you were younger. These wounds fester, preventing us from feeling whole, accepted, or loved. So we outsource the job of self-love to a number on a scale, one pants size smaller, or a quick fix in the form of a pint of ice cream or another glass of wine. When we do this, when we look for worthiness and acceptance outside of ourselves, whether we know it or not, we are surrendering our power to heal. We settle for breadcrumbs when we deserve the whole loaf.

This is one of the great illusions of human existence: This whole idea that what we desire exists outside ourselves is just completely false. The notion that our worth exists within the next career, relationship, paycheck, or friends who are just a little bit cooler than our current friends is the truly crazy thing. So cut it out, girl! Reclaim your power, own it, and allow your body to reflect the glow of the purity of your inner well-being, gratitude, and worth. When we strip all the noise away, we get to reveal what is true at the core. Love, acceptance, and connection always rise to the top.

The practice of breathwork allows us to remove the energetic noise that prevents us from living from this positive space. Our systems are operating from emotions that are decades old, or not even ours, because we often take on emotions of other people—often people we love—and claim them as our own. Once we come to learn that breathwork helps us to release these old emotions, we can become more present to what is right in front of us. We learn to lean on our breath in times of stress. We become less vulnerable to hijacking by stressful situations, less at the mercy of our circumstances, and less reactive. When we use breathwork we remove the emotional clutter that has built itself into our bodies so we are more grounded in times of stress. We can remember that we are okay, we have all we need already inside us, and we can rely on our breath to guide us through.

This breathwork practice, my friend, is a tool for you to access and step into your power, for you to access your intuition and reveal the truth of who you are. You can begin to make decisions based on the path that is right for you. Tapping into this calm center in your body removes the hustle, removes the list of pros and cons, removes the overanalyzing. You get to feel the truth of who you are and operate your life from that grounded place of clarity. You get to feel that peace. And you get to start right now.

INTEGRATIVE PRACTICE

How do you teach embodied wisdom through a medium like a book that can be read only with the logical mind? The beauty of this practice is that it's the body that does the work, not the mind. The best transformation is an embodied experience, which by definition can't really be taught with words alone.

When the body has a visceral shift, we transform more quickly and with more ease, and when we stop trying to think our way through life and we shift the body on a core level, we can stop simply surviving and start to thrive. But that doesn't mean we can discount the power that words have here, either. Certain words when said aloud during a practice like breathwork can help us to release energy during that embodied experience. And they can help us to integrate the visceral shift into our narrative understanding of how the world works. So for your integrative practice I want you to do the breathwork I have created for this book. This audio is specifically for opening up the body so we can feel deeper and heal the relationship between our minds and our bodies with our breath. Find the guided breathwork practice on my website, at hungryforhappiness.com/breathwork.

Meditation: Breathwork for Healing Stress and Anxiety

If you don't have Internet access right this second you can practice on your own with these instructions. Start by turning on some relaxing, calming music and lie on your back. The breathing technique is simple enough, but chances are you will find it a little bit challenging. Once you get into it, it will gradually become easier. We are going to start with a 10-minute introduction. Generally, the positive effects of breathwork begin around the 7-minute mark, so this will give you a nice window into what we are doing here and give you a chance to see how eventually a longer practice might be even more beneficial.

Get yourself a timer and some calming music, preferably without lyrics. The breathing exercise will feel a little bit difficult at first so practice the techniques a few times before turning your timer on. Start by taking two short breaths in through your nose and then pushing one long exhale out of your mouth. The first breath is into your solar plexus and the second is into your chest: Think of sending one breath into the bottom of your lungs, sending the other breath into the top of your lungs, then letting all of your breath out. In through the nose all the way to the belly, in through the nose to the chest, all the way out through the mouth. In, in, out. In, in, out.

Journaling: Body Correspondence

Okay, now that you have taken a moment to experience at least one breathwork exercise, I want you to write down everything you experienced while breathing. Whether it was in your mind or in your body, whether it was emotional or peaceful. Good, bad, or ugly, just write it all down. Here are some prompts to get you started:

1. How did I feel emotionally at the beginning of the exercise?

2. How did my body feel as I experienced this unusual breathing pattern?

3. Did my emotions or my thoughts change over the period of the breathwork exercise?

4. How did I feel once the exercise was over?

Make a decision not to be overly judgmental with yourself about your breathwork experience; it is a learning experience and it may take a few sessions to really fall into the rhythm of it. Allow this experience to just be—there is no need to make up a story about what it meant or judge yourself harshly if it didn't come to you naturally. I want you to be able to just be curious about this experience and let it remain a question in your mind as you carry on with your healing journey.

Often when we are healing, the beginning feels overwhelming. If you don't have a clear picture of this first experience with breathwork, I want to encourage you to give it a little space and try again. For the next few days, new ideas and new possibilities for meaning will arrive. When they do return to your journal and write them all down. Then start the exercise over again. Begin the breathwork exercise above or via the guided meditation link, and when it is over open your journal to answer the following questions:

1. How was your experience different this time?

2. What new insights did you have?

3. How did you feel at the beginning of the exercise?

4. How did you feel at the end of the exercise?

Breathwork is a practice. It is something that you can return to at any time, whenever you need it, or as a daily routine to start or end your day. If you are looking for more resources or guided breathwork practices, visit my website. I have been building resources since I discovered this amazing modality for health and healing.

CHAPTER 15

THE BEGINNING

Here we are at the end. But at the same time, we are very much at the beginning. This is the start of a new way of being in connection with your body and having a healthy relationship with the truth. The truth about your journey with food is that once you are in a communicative, connected relationship with your body, you can release your obsession with food and numbers on a scale. After all, it was never about the food or the shape of your body. It was always the relationship you have with your body and your emotions as they reside within it. Now is the time to release all the coping strategies that have kept you small. You no longer need them. It's time to release all the false limitations you have been clinging to. The good news is you have already done the work. All you need to do is keep at it.

The end of this book marks the beginning of your new relationship with your body, but that doesn't mean you won't struggle. I cannot guarantee smooth sailing from here. You can, however, remember the divine strength that resides inside you during those tough times that arise in the future. In the midst of your struggles and not-so-Instagram-able moments, on the verge of a binge or the temptation of starting a new diet, you can remember the strength that has gotten you to this point. It has always been there. In those moments when you want to reach for a crutch, remember to step into your power and be in a relationship with yourself and the body you live in.

Remember to observe that beautiful (often chaotic) mind of yours. Observe it with love and compassion. Thoughts arise. You can notice them, acknowledge them, and let them go. You are not your thoughts. They don't define you. They are just suggestions. Take what is useful. Leave the rest.

I want you to embody your sense of wonder and exploration. Don't wait to play. Don't wait to set yourself free in the playground of life. Express the essence of your inner child. Sing and dance, play and joke—life is far too short to not be joyful.

I want you to remember your magic—the part of you that is eager to emerge from the walls of protection you've built.

You have begun the work of embracing your darkness, the parts of you that you've been at war with, the parts you've desperately tried to hide from the world. These parts need healing. They need your love. They need you to show up for them.

These parts of you that may feel new or particularly vulnerable are the same ones you have been committed to silencing with food, and it's time to feel them—it's time to feel so you can heal.

Pain is your portal to your truth. Pain guides you to all the places that need the salve of your awareness, love, and compassion. Don't shy away. Lean in and love. By loving our pain and learning from it, we deepen the relationship with our body. Our body softens as we pay attention to her. She awakens in the wave of self-compassion.

There is no limit to the amount of joy we have access to. Joy isn't a privilege but a birthright. Savor the pleasures and deliciousness of your life. Extract the sweetness from life by appreciating the gifts. Pay attention to the things that bring you joy and you will find food to be one of them. You have the power to reclaim your joy around food. Allow this relationship to be your portal to the divine. Nourish your vessel with foods that awaken your soul and ignite your body with vibrant energy. Extract joy in the moments of presence. How good can you make it?

Expect miracles. Count on miracles as much as you count on your next breath. Embrace them with absolute certainty. Miracles are found within the simple moments of life, even the moments that may seem mundane. So don't overlook the ordinary or you'll miss the extraordinary it's hiding.

I want you to be captivated by your own courage—the voice that speaks up when your mind wants to give up and convince you that you aren't worthy. Lean into this courage. Let it guide you. Its force can overcome any obstacle that the mind convinces you is real.

Remember how safe you are in your body, safe to express all of who you are. You are safe to feel all you're meant to feel. Your nervous system is allowed to relax and surrender into deep rest, soul rest—the kind of rest that isn't achievable through sleep. Remember that in any moment you can give your body sips of this tender feeling. Simply speak softly to yourself, fall into the feeling of safety, and the world will appear brighter and your heart will feel softer.

And, of course, remember your breath. Breathe into your body and reacquaint yourself with it when things are difficult. Your breath can shift your mind-set when you're on the verge of a binge. Your breath can connect you back into your body and into your heart when it feels easy to shame your body. What a beautiful gift!

My heart is aching for your struggle and excited for your next chapter. I know the struggle you have been through. I know that in my moments of darkness, I didn't think it was possible to use food for health and hunger. I didn't think I would ever be in a place where I felt comfortable in my body.

On the other side of that place now, I feel like my life has been split into two. I remember my struggle with food and my body. But my understanding of myself and my understanding of my body are so very different now. It is almost as though I have an entirely new story. This new story is about joy and gratitude within my body. It has been such a joy to be able to share it with you—to have you on this journey with me. I am forever grateful for the opportunity to help to shift your world into one of deeper alignment.

You are the very thing you've been waiting for. There is nothing outside of yourself that will allow you to feel what you feel. Your answers exist nowhere except within you. The answers to all your desires are already there. Every sensation you need to feel is already there. It always has been. Your mission now is to experience it in its fullness and flavor.

Remember, these tools are always accessible. They are accessible when life gets noisy and events call for you to dive in and remember the truth.

Thank you for this honor and privilege. Thank you for trusting me, trusting yourself, and exploring a new way of being.

Together we rise.

INTEGRATIVE PRACTICE

Vision casting is one of my all-time favorite tools for manifestation. People all around the world use it because it is incredibly powerful. There is power in creating what we want for our future; it isn't enough to simply think positively. As we've learned, we have to feel our true power in our bodies. We have to tap into our visceral intelligence to really grasp what it is we truly want, and how we can make it happen for ourselves.

Meditation: Vision Casting

Close your eyes. Take a deep breath. Check in with your body. Listen for your connection to your body. Ask what it needs at this moment. How can I love you more? What is the vision you have for our future? Feel in your body for the vision you have of your future. How does your body want to feel in this future self? Ask your body for these answers.

Intent: What is it that you desire? What is your intention?

Visual: What does it look like? Is anyone there with you?

Visceral: What does it *feel* like? What is the sensation this creates in your body?

When you have a clear vision and feeling for this future, let it out into the universe to meet you back where you are right now.

Journaling: A Letter from Your Future Self

Now that you've completed the Hungry for Happiness journey, anchor in the transformation by creating your future self. You are going to write a letter from your future self to who you are today, explaining all that has changed and who you've become. Here are some sentences to get you started:

- I'm so excited to tell you how amazing life is . . .
- Each day I wake up feeling . . .
- I have completely let go of . . .
- Each day I am excited for . . .
- I'm so excited about . . .

Keep in mind the elements of vision casting as you flow through this exercise. Tap into your intention and understand what it looks like and how it feels in your body. When we tap into the frequency, we will attract the very things we desire without force or hustle. Allow yourself to write from a place of pure abundance, creativity, and possibility. You are the creator. Hold nothing back.

Thank you for practicing with me.
It has been such a pleasure.

ACKNOWLEDGMENTS

Nothing is self-made. Everything I create is fueled by the love, words, and hugs of those so close to me. These people are medicine to my nervous system on a daily basis. These people are the ones pulling me back down to earth and remembering to pay attention to the things that truly matter.

Eric: Thank you for being my soft place to land, and the one person in life I am committed to loving and annoying every day. Your ruthless support and seeing me, really seeing me, gives me life.

Mom & Dad: Thank you for constantly allowing me to fall apart in front of your eyes, while you wipe my tears and let me know I'm designed for this. You believed in me far before I believed in myself.

Chris & Britt: I adore you both. I got lucky in this life to have you by my side.

Dad & Jodi: Finding a felt sense of home and family in your presence is easy and effortless. Who knew belly laughs with parents was my favorite thing?

5BF: I don't know where to start. Love runs deep; forever bonded.

Hungry for Happiness & Pause Breathwork Team: You humans are the fuel to this mission. Thank you for your constant service and love for what we are all cocreating together.

The Hay House Family: Reid, Margarete, Patty, Allison, Bill, and Heidi. Thank you for seeing and believing in this book. Changing the world with you all is inspiring.

Lumies: The journey has just begun. Thank you for creating potent fields that allow me to constantly see the truth of life, the truth that exists within my soul when I surrender the narrative of my conditioning. I am forever grateful for the endless minis and tune-ups.

My soul sisters and brothers: Ya'll know who you are. Knowing your hearts are on the other side of a FaceTime reminds me we are all walking each other home, day in and day out. Journeying with you in this life is fun, expansive, and supportive.

God/Life Force Energy/Universe: Whatever words we wanna slap on this most powerful yet invisible force present. I feel your nudges, thank you for dropping into my soul what needs to be created for this world. Thank you for allowing me to be the vessel for these messages.

To my younger self: Thank you for riding the waves of emotionality, sifting through the oceans of chaos. You are a strong, ruthless, and committed cookie. I wouldn't be here without your strength to never stop asking, growing, questioning the narrative, and never giving up.

ABOUT THE AUTHOR

Samantha Skelly is an entrepreneur, motivational speaker, author, breathwork facilitator, and emotional eating expert. In 2014, she founded Hungry for Happiness to support women around the world battling disordered eating and body image issues. In 2018 she founded Pause Breathwork, a movement to decrease the suffering humanity experiences though the power of breathwork. She continues to spread her message through her programs, international retreats, motivational speaking engagements, and podcast. Samantha is Canadian and now lives between the mountains and beach in Southern California.

Visit her online www.hungryforhappinesss.com and on Instagram @samanthaskelly.

Hay House Titles of Related Interest

YOU CAN HEAL YOUR LIFE, the movie,
starring Louise Hay & Friends
(available as a 1-DVD program, an expanded 2-DVD set,
and an online streaming video)
Learn more at hayhouse.com/louise-movie

THE SHIFT, the movie, starring Dr. Wayne W. Dyer
(available as a 1-DVD program, an expanded 2-DVD set,
and an online streaming video)
Learn more at hayhouse.com/the-shift-movie

*THE HEALTH HABIT: 7 Easy Steps to Reach Your Goals and
Dramatically Improve Your Life,* by Elizabeth Rider

*HUNGRY FOR MORE: Satisfy Your Deepest Cravings,
Feed Your Dreams and Live a Full-Up Life,* by Mel Wells

All of the above are available at your local bookstore,
or may be ordered by contacting Hay House (see next page).

We hope you enjoyed this Hay House book. If you'd like to receive our online catalog featuring additional information on Hay House books and products, or if you'd like to find out more about the Hay Foundation, please contact:

Hay House, Inc., P.O. Box 5100, Carlsbad, CA 92018-5100
(760) 431-7695 or (800) 654-5126
(760) 431-6948 (fax) or (800) 650-5115 (fax)
www.hayhouse.com® • www.hayfoundation.org

———

Published in Australia by: Hay House Australia Pty. Ltd.,
18/36 Ralph St., Alexandria NSW 2015
Phone: 612-9669-4299 • *Fax:* 612-9669-4144
www.hayhouse.com.au

Published in the United Kingdom by: Hay House UK, Ltd.,
The Sixth Floor, Watson House, 54 Baker Street, London W1U 7BU
Phone: +44 (0)20 3927 7290 • *Fax:* +44 (0)20 3927 7291
www.hayhouse.co.uk

Published in India by: Hay House Publishers India,
Muskaan Complex, Plot No. 3, B-2, Vasant Kunj, New Delhi 110 070
Phone: 91-11-4176-1620 • *Fax:* 91-11-4176-1630
www.hayhouse.co.in

———

Access New Knowledge.
Anytime. Anywhere.

Learn and evolve at your own pace
with the world's leading experts.

www.hayhouseU.com

Listen. Learn. Transform.

Listen to the audio version of this book for FREE!

Today, life is more hectic than ever—so you deserve on-demand and on-the-go solutions that inspire growth, center your mind, and support your well-being.

Introducing the *Hay House Unlimited Audio* mobile app. Now you can listen to this book (and countless others)—without having to restructure your day.

With your membership, you can:

- Enjoy over 30,000 hours of audio from your favorite authors.

- Explore audiobooks, meditations, Hay House Radio episodes, podcasts, and more.

- Listen anytime and anywhere with offline listening.

- Access exclusive audios you won't find anywhere else.

Try FREE for 7 days!

Visit **hayhouse.com/unlimited** to start your free trial and get one step closer to living your best life.